Endorsements

"The celebration of Canada's 150th anniversary in 2017 was a poignant reminder that, as Christians, we ought to thank God for past blessings while entreating him for future mercies. The present volume provides an insightful analysis of the reasons behind both. It is a collection of essays, in which the authors trace the dramatic shifts in the history of Protestantism in Ontario, highlight the significant changes that have occurred in Canadian society in recent decades, establish a solid biblical/theological framework for understanding the relationship between church and state, and provide pastoral insight into how we ought to perceive our role as Christians in Canada. All told, this book is a timely gift to God's people as it assures us that nations rise and fall while Christ's church remains, and it reminds us to embrace our principle calling—namely, to live out our identity in Christ to the glory of God among the nations."

J. Stephen Yuille
Vice President of Academics and
Academic Dean of College, Heritage College & Seminary;
Associate Professor of Biblical Spirituality,
The Southern Baptist Theological Seminary

"*Desiring a Better Country* is essential reading for Canadian Christians. It has challenged me, encouraged me and made me feel connected with the big story of what God is doing in this land."

Andrew Fountain
Pastor of Newlife Church, Toronto;
Former Principal of Toronto Baptist Seminary

"This book is a vital read for every pastor in Canada. It will help you understand the soil in which you are working and assist you in gaining a theological framework to think through how the church should live as salt and light in our beloved country. It will be my go-to resource to give to new pastors and faithful church members who desire to understand the water in which they swim."

Paul W. Martin
Pastor of Grace Fellowship Church, Toronto

"If Canada is now post-Christian, as many observers believe, then the question must be asked—when *was* it ever Christian? Not only do the contributors of *Desiring a Better Country* offer striking evidence of the spiritual vitality of Canadian Christian witness in the nineteenth century, but they also helpfully trace how such a rich heritage was lost in favour of the secularizing trends of the twentieth century. These authors' biblically grounded hope for the future is that Christians will learn from the past. Canadian pastors, and all concerned Evangelicals, will find in this book a history they have forgotten; namely, their own."

Clint Humfrey
Senior Pastor, Calvary Grace Church, Calgary, Alberta

Desiring a Better Country
150 Years of Christian Witness in Canada:
Legacy & Relevance

Desiring
A BETTER COUNTRY

150 Years of Christian Witness in Canada: Legacy and Relevance

Kevin N. Flatt • Michael A.G. Haykin • Glendon G. Thompson

Kirk Wellum • Stephen J. Wellum

Edited by
Chance Faulkner, Michael A.G. Haykin and Corey M.K. Hughes

H&E
Publishing

Desiring a Better Country: 150 Years of Christian Witness in Canada: Legacy & Relevance

Copyright © 2020 H&E Publishing

All rights reserved. This book or any portion thereof may not be reproduced or used in any manner whatsoever without the express written permission of the publisher except for the use of brief quotations in a book review.

Published by: H&E Publishing, Peterborough, Ontario
www.hesedandemet.com

Paperback ISBN: 978-1-7752633-1-9
ePub ISBN: 978-1-989174-14-2
Revised Edition, 2020

Contents

Preface ix

1. Sit Lux: Evangelicalism in Ontario, 1790s–1890s 1
   Michael A. G Haykin

2. A Century of Change: Protestantism in Canada in the Twentieth Century 31
   Kevin N. Flatt

3. Church and State: Gospel Imperatives 63
   Kirk Wellum

4. Church and State: Theological Perspectives 87
   Stephen J. Wellum

5. Desiring a Better Country 119
   Glendon G. Thompson

Contributors 129

Scripture Index 131

Preface

The essays in this slim volume originated as papers given at a two-day conference held at Jarvis Street Baptist Church, Toronto, in October of 2017. This well-attended conference, which was designed to coincide with the sesquicentennial year of Canada's nationhood, sought to reflect on where we have been in terms of the Christian Faith as a nation and what place Christianity has in the future of Canadians as a people. Ever since the 1960s Canadian historians have downplayed the vital role that Christianity played in the lives of many men and women who built this nation before and after Confederation (for more detail, see my own essay below). For instance, the textbook that I had in Grade 13 Canadian History in the early 1970s at Ancaster High and Vocational School—K. A. MacKirdy, J. S. Moir and Y. F, Zoltvany, ed., *Changing Perspectives in Canadian History: Selected Problems*—gave almost nary a hint about the way Christianity was woven into the fabric of Anglophone and Francophone life in this land. Granted there has been a massive sea-change since the 1960s (well discussed below by Kevin Flatt), but any discussion of the history of Canadian identity cannot ignore this fact.

But then, where are we going as a Canadian people? Given Augustine's dictum that nations are ruled by what they love and desire, what is it that will shape the hearts and minds of Canadians in the days to come? Three essays—those by Kirk and Stephen Wellum and the sermon by Glendon Thompson—seek to answer this question in what is undoubtedly a thought-provoking manner. Despite the demographic changes that have taken place in Canada regarding Christianity, all of the authors of this book are convinced that the Christian Faith still has a key contribution to make in both the public square and private sector of Canadian life. Read and reflect—and pray!

Michael A.G. Haykin
Dundas, Ontario
October 2, 2018.

1
Sit Lux:
Evangelicalism in Ontario, 1790s–1890s

Michael A.G. Haykin

In 1994 Queen Elizabeth II approved a slight change to the Canadian coat of arms, which had been formally adopted seventy years earlier. A red annulus or circular ribbon was added behind the coat of arms on which the Latin phrase, *Desiderantes meliorem patriam* "They desire a better country," was placed in capital letters. The phrase is a clear allusion to Hebrews 11:16, though the Latin is not that of the Vulgate. In its original context Hebrews 11:16 is an eschatological text that attributes to the Jewish patriarchs a life-long orientation towards a heavenly country or city whose builder was God, an orientation that also profoundly shaped how they lived in this world. In the context of the Canadian coat of arms, the passage is probably a secularized referent to the many immigrants who have come to this country seeking a better life and a better world than the one they had left behind.

And yet this biblical allusion is indeed apropos for the Canadian coat of arms since it is an important reminder of the vital impact that Evangelical Christianity has exercised in this nation, described by historian Michael Gauvreau as a "creative role in shaping cultural traditions, social forms, and political ideologies."[1] Gauvreau and his wife Nancy Christie are convinced that it was the Christian Faith "rather than social and economic structures, that constituted the central dynamic of community formation" in British North America.[2]

Peter H. Russell has argued in his recent work *Canada's Odyssey: A Country Based on Incomplete Conquests* that this nation's identity rests on three pillars: Aboriginal Canada, French Canada, and English Canada. A complete study of the impact of Christianity on this nation should thus take account of the way this faith has shaped each of these pillars.[3] What follows has a more modest goal: it looks at the impact of Evangelicalism upon one area of English Canada, namely, the province of Ontario, also known as Upper Canada and Canada West, from the 1790s to the 1890s.

---

[1] Michael Gauvreau, "Beyond the Half-Way House: Evangelicalism and the Shaping of English Canadian Culture," *Acadiensis*, 20, no.2 (Spring 1991): 158. John G. Stackhouse, Jr makes the same point with regard to twentieth-century Evangelicalism in his "'Who Whom?' Evangelicalism and Canadian Society" in G. A. Rawlyk, ed., *Aspects of the Canadian Evangelical Experience* (Montreal, QC & Kingston, ON/London/Buffalo, NY: McGill-Queen's University Press, 1997), 60–63.

[2] Nancy Christie and Michael Gauvreau, *Christian Churches and Their Peoples, 1849-1965: A Social History of Religion in Canada* (Toronto, ON/Buffalo, NY/London: University of Toronto Press, 2010), 10. Canadian sociologist S. D. Clark (1910-2003) has similarly noted: "In few countries in the western world has religion exerted as great an influence upon the development of the community as it has in Canada" (cited Goldwin French, "The Evangelical Creed in Canada" in W. L. Morton, ed., *The Shield of Achilles* [Toronto, ON/Montreal, QC: McClelland and Stewart Ltd., 1968], 15).

[3] Peter H. Russell, *Canada's Odyssey: A Country Based on Incomplete Conquests* (Toronto, ON/Buffalo, NY/London: University of Toronto Press, 2017).

"A vocal and aggressive evangelicalism"

In the very decades of the nineteenth century and early twentieth century when the society, ideologies, and institutions of Ontario were being formed, Evangelicalism was *the* dominant form of Christianity. For example, if we combine the percentages of the Ontario population that were Methodists, Presbyterians, and Baptists, the three largest Evangelical denominations, then we have the following statistics between 1842 and 1901:[4]

1842	1861	1871	1881	1891	1901	1911
46.4	60.6	55.8	57.9	57.3	57.7	52.7

Nor do these figures include the Evangelical wing of the Anglican Church. This was a sizeable body within Ontarian Anglicanism, which comprised some 26.4% of the population of Ontario in 1861, though by 1901 this had declined to 16.9%.[5] In 1862, Francis Fulford (1803–1868), the Anglo-Catholic Bishop of Montreal, reckoned that Evangelicals "occupied the cathedral of Toronto [that is, St. James'], all the churches of Kingston,...one in Hamilton, and the church at London."[6] Two prominent

---

[4] For these statistics, see John Webster Grant, *A Profusion of Spires: Religion in Nineteenth-Century Ontario* (Toronto, ON/Buffalo, NY/London: University of Toronto Press, 1988), 224; Michael Gauvreau, "Protestantism Transformed: Personal Piety and the Evangelical Social Vision, 1815–1867" in George A. Rawlyk, ed., *The Canadian Protestant Experience 1760 to 1990* (Burlington, ON: Welch Publishing Co., 1990), 96; Phyllis D. Airhart, "Ordering a New Nation and Reordering Protestantism 1867–1914" in Rawlyk, ed., *Canadian Protestant Experience*, 103.

[5] Gauvreau, "Protestantism Transformed," 96; Airhart, "Ordering a New Nation and Reordering Protestantism," 103.

[6] Cited Richard W. Vaudry, "Evangelical Anglicans and the Atlantic World: Politics, Ideology, and the British North American

Canadian historians, William Westfall of York University and Phyllis D. Airhart, Professor of the History of Christianity at Emmanuel College, have maintained that up until the turn of the twentieth century, the Anglican Church in Canada was profoundly influenced by Evangelicalism.[7]

Yet, it bears remembering that, although Evangelical Anglicans and their fellow Evangelicals in Methodism, Presbyterianism, or Baptist circles, had, in the words of the staunch Tory John Strachan (1778-1867), the first Anglican bishop of Toronto, "the same objects in view," namely, the "extension of Christ's kingdom,"[8] there was often little contact between the Anglicans and other Evangelicals. The ministerial leadership of the former had often been formally educated in English or Irish universities, which gave them a sense of superiority with regard to Methodist and Baptist preachers, who often had little formal theological education. The Anglican leadership was also in substantial agreement with the social stratification that prevailed in the British Isles, which for many of them was the touchstone by which to measure Canadian society and culture. The English feminist travel writer Anna Jameson (1794-1860) certainly spoke for some of these Anglicans when she stated in 1838:

Connection" in Rawlyk, ed., *Aspects of the Canadian Evangelical Experience*, 157.

[7] William Westfall, *Two Worlds: The Protestant Culture of Nineteenth-Century Ontario* (Kingston, ON/Montreal, QC: McGill-Queen's University Press, 1989) and Phyllis D. Airhart, *Serving the Present Age: Revivalism, Progressivism, and the Methodist Tradition in Canada* (Montreal, QC/Kingston, ON: McGill-Queen's University Press, 1992).

[8] Cited Goldwin S. French, "The Impact of Christianity on Canadian Culture and Society before 1867," *Theological Bulletin*, 3 (January 1968): 20.

> Canada is a colony, not a country; it is not yet identified with the dearest affections and associations, remembrances, and hopes of its inhabitants: it is to them an adopted, not a real mother. Their love, their pride, are not for poor Canada, but for high and happy England...[9]

And that "high and happy England" was a world of marked social distinctions, in which the leadership as well as the rank and file of Evangelical groups like the Methodists and Baptists nearly always ranked lower on the social scale than that of the Anglicans.[10]

Nor do the statistics cited above include some smaller Evangelical communities, like the Plymouth Brethren and those among the Lutherans and Mennonites.[11] All told, it would not be a stretch to estimate that by the close of the nineteenth century close to 70% of Ontarians were sitting regularly under an Evangelical ministry. It is also noteworthy that in 1842, 16.7% of Ontarians professed no commitment to Christianity in any shape or form. By 1901, this had declined to 0.5%![12] At the height of their influence, between the 1850s and the 1910s, the Evangelicals organized alliances for direct political action, "formed

---

[9] Anna Jameson, *Winter Studies and Summer Rambles in Canada* (London: Saunders and Otley, 1838), I, 100.

[10] French, "Impact of Christianity on Canadian Culture and Society," 20-21.

[11] On Evangelicalism among Canadian Lutherans, see Bryan V. Hillis, "Lutheranism and Evangelicalism: Travelling in the Same Circle of Influence" in Rawlyk, ed., *Aspects of the Canadian Evangelical Experience*, 241-254; and for Evangelicalism among the Mennonites, see Bruce L. Guenther, "Living with the Virus: The Enigma of Evangelicalism among Mennonites in Canada" in Rawlyk, ed., *Aspects of the Canadian Evangelical Experience*, 223-240.

[12] Grant, *Profusion of Spires*, 224.

missionary societies, fought slavery, encouraged education, founded hospitals for the sick, asylums for the insane, and urged temperance and civic reform."[13] In a word, as Marguerite van Die has stated: "Ontario in the nineteenth century was the heartland of a vocal and aggressive evangelicalism."[14]

"A dismal region of moral darkness"

At the beginning of European settlement in Upper Canada, however, the situation was quite different. "A dismal region of moral darkness and the shadow of death" where most families had "no books, not even a Bible," and were "grossly ignorant" was the way that the American Calvinistic Baptist missionary Asahel Morse (1771-1838) described Upper Canadian society in the first decade of the nineteenth century.[15] Morse's perspective is undoubtedly shaped by the fact that he was the product of a longline of preachers—his father, for example, had been converted under the preaching of George Whitefield (1714-1770)—and that he could never remember a time when he was unable to read.[16] Yet, other testimonies from this era in Upper Canadian history echo similar sentiments. The prominent Methodist revivalist Nathan Bangs (1778-1862), who ministered for twelve

---

[13] Margaret Conrad, Alvin Finkel, and Cornelius J. Jaenen, *History of the Canadian Peoples* (Toronto, ON: Copp Clark Pitman Ltd., 1993), 1:559.

[14] Marguerite van Die, "'The Double Vision': Evangelical Piety as Derivative and Indigenous in Victorian English Canada" in Mark A. Noll, David W. Bebbington, and George A. Rawlyk, ed., *Evangelicalism: Comparative Studies of Popular Protestantism in North America, the British Isles, and Beyond, 1700-1900* (New York/Oxford: Oxford University Press, 1994), 254.

[15] Stuart Ivison and Fred Rosser, *The Baptists in Upper and Lower Canada before 1820* (Toronto: University of Toronto Press, 1956), 52-53.

[16] Ivison and Rosser, *Baptists in Upper and Lower Canada*, 76-77.

years in both Upper and Lower Canada, remembered the inhabitants of York in 1801, for example, as "thoughtless and wicked as the Canaanites of old."[17] The Anglican bishop John Strachan similarly observed of the people of York: "The majority had little or no sense of religion."[18]

Asahel Morse attributed this situation of moral depression to the fact that nearly all of the inhabitants of Upper Canada were recent immigrants who had arrived after the close of the American Revolution.[19] By 1791, for instance, Upper Canada alone had received approximately 10,000 such immigrants. These early pioneers were followed by an equally large number in the following decade who came to take advantage of a proclamation of free land for new settlers that was issued on February 7, 1792 by the first lieutenant-governor of Upper Canada, John Graves Simcoe (1752–1806).

These new immigrants had to brave what one writer called Upper Canada's "inclement climate privations."[20] The physical challenges of gospel ministry in the colony are well captured in the following description of John Winterbotham (c.1795–1868), one-time pastor of the First Baptist Church in Brantford and the editor of *The Christian Messenger*, a forerunner of *The Canadian Baptist*, about the founding of the Baptist cause at Vittoria. Winterbotham notes that in the 1790s the area around Vittoria was "almost an unbroken forest, having only a very few human habitations scattered here and there in the thick woods down to the shore of Long Point Bay." American Baptist

---

[17] Cited Abel Stevens, *Life and Times of Nathan Bangs, D.D.* (New York: Carlton & Porter, 1863), 361.

[18] Cited Grant, *Profusion of Spires*, 52.

[19] Ivison and Rosser, *Baptists in Upper and Lower Canada*, 52–53.

[20] Stevens, *Life and Times of Nathan Bangs*, 73.

missionaries seeking to plant Baptist works in the new country, Winterbotham continues:

> had to traverse the country all the way from Niagara River to Long Point, across swamps, over rivers and creeks, and through trackless woods, thus evincing their love for the souls of dying men. Meetings had been held... in log barns and houses, and when the weather permitted under the shade of lofty trees, whose huge branches screened the humble worshipers from the scorching rays of the sun.[21]

Except for such ethnic religious groups as the Mennonites, who created homogeneous communities on the new frontier, these new settlers had to forge anew the bonds of community and religious life. It is no wonder that such a fluid situation meant also the disintegration of traditional bonds of moral and religious order.

"Pleading with sinners... seemed to melt every heart"
One Evangelical Christian community that was well-prepared to take on the challenge of this religious vacuum were the Methodists. Ideally suited to minister in a largely unsettled frontier context of isolated communities, Methodism especially relied upon a combination of itinerant clergymen—the famous black-robed circuit riders—and local lay exhorters. These lay exhorters kept the fires of Methodist piety burning in local class meetings between the visits of such dynamic and intense preachers as William Losee (1757-1832), Lorenzo Dow (1777-1834), Nathan Bangs, and William Case (1780-1855). Losee's preaching, typical of Methodist sermons of this era, was, according to one

---

[21] "Valedictory Services at Vittoria," *The Christian Messenger*, 1, no.35 (May 31, 1855).

writer, "more hortatory than expository. He was impassioned, voluble, fearless, and denunciatory, cutting deep and closely, and praying God to 'smite sinners.'"[22] Although Methodism grew more slowly in towns, where it had to compete with other church bodies, they were without rivals in rural Upper Canada and, by the War of 1812-1815, formed the largest Christian denomination in Upper Canada.[23] A rough estimate would place the total number of Methodist members and adherents at that time between 20,000 and 26,000, in the range of 28 to 34% of the entire population of Upper Canada.

This pattern of significant growth continued unabated for much of the nineteenth century. Thus, in 1861, Methodists were still the largest denomination in Ontario with 29.7% of the total population, while the Anglicans had 26.4% and the Presbyterians 25.7%. By 1891, Ontario Methodists boasted 30.9% of the population of the province, with the Presbyterians at 21.4% and the Anglicans at 18.3%.[24]

A central vehicle in this growth of Methodism during the first third of the nineteenth century was the rural camp meeting. After the 1837 rebellion, though, travelling Methodist evangelists like James Caughey (*c*.1810-1891)—an Irishman who had been converted in the United States—and Phoebe Palmer

---

[22] Cited Neil Semple, *The Lord's Dominion: The History of Canadian Methodism* (Montreal, QC/Kingston, ON: McGill-Queen's University Press, 1996), 43.

[23] Nancy Christie, "'In These Times of Democratic Rage and Delusion': Popular Religion and the Challenge to the Established Order, 1760-1815" in Rawlyk, ed., *Canadian Protestant Experience 1760 to 1990*, 22-23.

[24] For these statistics, see Gauvreau, "Protestantism Transformed," 96 and Airhart, "Ordering a New Nation and Reordering Protestantism," 103. See also Daniel C. Goodwin, "'The Footprints of Zion's King': Baptists in Canada to 1880" in Rawlyk, ed., *Aspects of the Canadian Evangelical Experience*, 196-197.

(1807-1874) preferred to hold large mass meetings in urban centres. Caughey preached standard Wesleyan Methodist theology: the universal need for conversion along with the offer of Christian perfection, which, according to the Methodist patriarch, John Wesley (1703-1791), was the second stage of the Christian life. Caughey's Methodist theology and revivalist spirituality was yoked to tremendous oratorical gifts and an innate ability to read a congregation.[25]

In November 1851 Caughey came to Toronto, where he stayed for nearly eight months and preached seven sermons a week during his time there. During this time the membership of the Wesleyan Methodist churches in the city grew from 714 to 1,537. It is obvious that a good number of people outside of Methodist circles were also affected by his preaching, since some 2,000 people were converted during his stay. In the fall of 1852 he visited Kingston. His impact there was similar to the one he had had in Toronto: both Wesleyan Methodist and Baptist membership grew at unprecedented rates. Then, over the course of the academic year 1852-1853, he spoke at Victoria College, Cobourg. This institution had been founded in 1836 as Upper Canada Academy; the name was changed in 1841 to Victoria College. Prior to his coming, less than 25% of the students there were professing Christians. Afterwards a mere 5% were not.[26] In March of 1853 he came to Hamilton, arriving in time to help speed a revival that was already in process. The Wesleyan Methodist minister in Hamilton, John Saltkill Carroll (1809-1884)—

---

[25] Peter Bush, "Caughey, James," *Dictionary of Canadian Biography* (http://www.biographi.ca/en/bio/caughey_james_12E.html; accessed October 5, 2017).

[26] George A. Rawlyk, *Wrapped Up in God: A Study of Several Canadian Revivals and Revivalists* (Burlington, ON: Welch Publishing Co., 1988), 103-107.

whose middle name derived from the New Brunswick island on which he was born and which he apparently never used[27]—was thrilled to have him preach and the membership doubled as a result of Caughey's three-and-a-half-month ministry.

Presbyterian historian Peter Bush identified at least two lasting marks Caughey left on Canadian Evangelicalism.[28] The ministry of Caughey increased the openness of Canadian Evangelicals to the Holiness movement and as such opened the door to the Pentecostal movement at the beginning of the twentieth century. Second, as a result of Caughey's ministry in Hamilton in 1853, a group of young men decided to become Wesleyan Methodist ministers. They went to Victoria College, Cobourg, and within a year a revival had broken out among the students there. Two men who would shape the contours of Canadian Methodism beyond the turn of the century in Ontario were deeply impacted by this revival: Albert Carman (1833-1917), who was converted in the revival, and Nathanael Burwash (1839-1918), who was profoundly shaped by it.[29]

It is also noteworthy that Caughey's preaching style was quiet, even somewhat scholarly—quite different from the ardent emotionalism at the camp meetings typified by William Losee earlier in the century. And yet, those who heard Caughey's sermons later commented that they possessed "great power" and his "pleading with sinners... seemed to melt every heart" of his audience.[30] Over the course of the next half century, conversion

---

[27] John Webster Grant, "Carroll, John Saltkill," *Dictionary of Canadian Biography* (http://www.biographi.ca/en/bio/carroll_john_saltkill_11E.html; accessed October 5, 2017).

[28] Bush, "Caughey, James."

[29] On Burwash, see Marguerite Van Die, *An evangelical mind: Nathanael Burwash and the Methodist tradition in Canada, 1839-1918* (Kingston, ON: McGill-Queen's University Press, 1989).

[30] Rawlyk, *Wrapped Up in God*, 105-106.

was still stressed in Methodist circles, but increasingly becoming a Christian was seen as a quiet process, somewhat like going through a tunnel with the light at the other end increasingly flooding one's sight until one emerges into daylight again. This shift among Methodists from revivalist ardour to order was ultimately due to two main factors: a growing desire for respectability and a desire to create a new social order.

"Christ would have been more honoured"

Though equally Evangelical, Baptist life in nineteenth-century Ontario presents a sharp contrast with Methodism. At the outbreak of the War of 1812–1815, which firmly cemented the bonds of Britain and her North American colonies, the Baptist community was little more than embryonic.[31] By that time fourteen churches had been founded, nearly all of them planted along the shores of either Lake Ontario or Lake Erie.[32] These churches had some 400 members and were linked together in two fledgling associations.[33] The Thurlow Association, which had been formed in 1802, consisted mostly of churches between Cobourg and Kingston. The Clinton Conference, formally a part of the powerful Shaftesbury Association of Vermont, New York, and New Hampshire until 1819, was made up of four churches—Charlotteville (Vittoria),[34] Townsend (Boston), Clinton (Beam-

---

[31] For a good account of this period in Ontario Baptist History, see Ivison and Rosser, *Baptists in Upper and Lower Canada*.

[32] For these churches, see Ivison and Rosser, *Baptists in Upper and Lower Canada*, 82–120.

[33] G. A. Rawlyk, *The Canada Fire: Radical Evangelicalism in British North America, 1775–1812* (Kingston & Montreal: McGill-Queen's University Press, 1994), 122.

[34] Of all the Baptist churches in Ontario the Vittoria church had the oldest continuous existence until it closed recently in 2013. See

sville), and Oxford (later Thames Street Baptist Church, Ingersoll). Each of the Baptist causes in these two associations was the result of extensive missionary efforts on the part of a number of American Calvinistic Baptist Associations.

A shared ecclesial tradition rooted in Calvinistic soteriology and the practice of closed communion thus united these early pioneer churches.[35] Such a common doctrinal heritage, though, does not appear to have resulted in significant numerical growth during this early period of Baptist witness in Ontario. Now, the Baptists were not a whit less Evangelical than their Methodist contemporaries. Like the Methodists, they were deeply committed to a conversionist faith—though they rejected the Methodist understanding of Christian perfection. Along with the Methodists, they were deeply biblicistic. And like the Methodists, they were ardent about being active for Christ in evangelism and good works.[36] What explanation, then, can be given for the significant disparity in their growth over the nineteenth century?

Daniel C. Goodwin has suggested that the Methodist use of the camp meeting as a key evangelistic tool in Upper Canada "goes a long way in explaining the denomination's phenomenal

---

Monte Sonnenberg, "Vittoria Baptists vote to disband," *Simcoe Reformer* (July 30, 2013) (http://www.simcoereformer.ca/2013/07/30/vittoria-baptists-vote-to-disband; accessed October 5, 2017).

[35] For a detailed development of this point, see William Norman Albert Gillespie, "Ontario's 19th Century Baptist Tradition: Its Roots and its Development" (PhD thesis, University of Waterloo, 1990), and *idem*, "The Recovery of Ontario's Baptist Tradition" in David T. Priestley, ed., *Memory and Hope: Strands of Canadian Baptist History* (Waterloo, ON: Wilfrid Laurier University Press, 1996), 25–37.

[36] Here I am utilizing elements of the famous Bebbington quadrilateral that many historians have employed as a way of defining Evangelicalism. See David Bebbington, *Evangelicalism in Modern Britain. A History from the 1730s to the 1980s* (1989 ed.; repr. Grand Rapids: Baker Book House, 1992).

growth and religious hegemony" in the first half of the nineteenth century.[37] Some historians point out that just as significant in the early years of Upper Canada's existence was the fact that Baptists in North America had by and large identified themselves with the American Revolution and therefore were generally not interested in coming to Upper Canada where they would once again be subject to the threat of oppression by an Established Church.[38]

Numerous historians of nineteenth-century Upper Canadian Baptist history, however, have opted for yet a third explanation for the slenderness of Baptist growth in the nineteenth century as compared with that of the Methodists. The American Baptist tradition of closed communion constituted the earliest Baptist witness in Upper Canada. But shortly after the close of the War of 1812-1815, open-communion Scottish Baptists began to emigrate to the Ottawa Valley and so introduced a tradition at odds with that of their American cousins. The conflict between these two groups of Baptists proved to be so divisive and lasted so far into the century, so this explanation runs, that it scuttled any attempt to establish a unified base for advance and evangelism.[39]

This explanation, though, has some inherent problems. It fails, for instance, to take into account the fact that "open" communionists were distinctly in the minority throughout the

---

[37] Daniel C. Goodwin, "The Footprints of Zion's King," 196-197.

[38] Winthrop S. Hudson, "Baptists, the Pilgrim Fathers, and the American Revolution" in his *Baptists in Transition: Individualism and Christian Responsibility* (Valley Forge, PA: Judson Press, 1979), 76-81; Gillespie, "Ontario's 19th Century Baptist Tradition," 99-100.

[39] For a detailed description of this historiographical tradition, see Gillespie, "Ontario's 19th Century Baptist Tradition," 1-91, *passim*.

nineteenth century and hardly in a position to impede a movement towards union.[40] Even in the Ottawa Valley, the heartland of the open communion point of view, there were relatively few of this persuasion. In fact, in the mid-1850s the Ottawa Association could describe itself as composed of churches which were "Calvinistic in doctrine, and close communion in practice."[41] And some of the leading figures in the early years of the Ottawa Association, men like the Scottish Baptist William Fraser (1801–1883), an intrepid evangelist,[42] had begun their ministries in Ontario as proponents of open communion and had over the course of time become firmly convinced of closed communion.[43]

Nineteenth-century Baptist individualism might also be considered as a key reason for the poor showing of Baptists in nineteenth-century Ontario. Especially under the impress of the writings of influential theologians like the Northern Baptist Francis Wayland (1796–1865), Baptists in Ontario, like their cousins in the United States, began to lose touch with "the early

---

[40] See Gillespie, "Ontario's 19th Century Baptist Tradition," 386-411.

[41] See Gillespie, "Ontario's 19th Century Baptist Tradition," 392-395. The quote is from the *Minutes of the Ottawa Baptist Association* (1856): 4, cited Gillespie, "Ontario's 19th Century Baptist Tradition," 395.

[42] For Fraser, see Michael A.G. Haykin, "Voluntarism in the Life and Ministry of William Fraser (1801-1883)" in William H. Brackney, ed., *The Believers Church: A Voluntary Church. Papers of the Twelfth Believers Church Conference held at McMaster Divinity College, October 17-19, 1996* (Kitchener, ON: Pandora Press, 1998), 25-50.

[43] See, for example, William Fraser, "From the Back-Woods," *The Christian Messenger*, 2, no.16 (January 17, 1856): 2, cols.5-7 and his "Open Communion and its Effects," *The Christian Messenger*, 3, no.7 (November 13, 1856): 2, cols.4-6. Also see "Open Communion Baptists in Canada," *The Christian Messenger*, 1, no.44 (August 2, 1855): 2, cols. 5-6: "The overwhelming majority of the Baptists of this fair Province are *Regular* Baptists."

connectionalism which had Baptists together in associations" in both the British Isles and colonial America. Instead, the contention began to be made that local churches are independent democracies and that "it was both wrong and dangerous to speak of the 'interdependence' of churches."[44] As one Baptist later said in 1853 about the negative impact that this rugged individualism had had upon early Baptist life:

> Had the Baptists of Canada laid aside their mutual jealousies at an earlier day, and concentrated their strength in aggressive movements upon the domains of sin and error, not only would our denominational statistics have reached a higher figure, but what is of infinitely more importance, Christ would have been more honoured by us...[45]

Yet another reason that could be mentioned for the struggles of the Baptists to establish themselves in Ontario would be their lack of commitment to theological education. As noted, the Methodists had established Upper Canada Academy in 1836. And in 1841, the Church of Scotland founded Queen's University, to be followed three years later by Knox College, established by congregations who sided with the Free Church of Scotland in the massive schism in the Church of Scotland in 1843. But it would not be until 1860, close to eighty years after Baptists had first come into Ontario, that they would have a successful school for training pastors, what was known as the Canadian Literary

---

[44] Norman H. Maring, "The Individualism of Francis Wayland" in Winthrop Still Hudson, ed., *Baptist Concepts of the Church: A Survey of the Historical and Theological Issues which Have Produced Changes in Church Order* (Philadelphia, PA: Judson Press, 1959), 136.

[45] "Regular Baptist Missionary Society," *The Christian Observer*, 3, no.11 (November 1853): 168.

Institute in Woodstock. There had been an earlier attempt, Canada Baptist College in Montreal, but it had failed in 1849 after only eleven years of operation.[46]

"Let there be light"

In the decade that followed the demise of the Canada Baptist College, there were some Baptists who did not lose sight of the importance of having a theological school in Ontario. After a couple of false starts, eight Baptist leaders, including Robert Alexander Fyfe (1816-1878), a Scottish-Canadian Baptist from the Ottawa Valley and the pastor of Bond Street Baptist Church in Toronto, met in mid-October, 1856 and issued a call for a convention to meet in Brantford on November 19 of that year to decide on the issue.[47] When the convention did meet, there were not as many Baptists there as was hoped, but a commitment was made for the establishment of a school to be located not "east of St. Catherines" nor "west of London."[48] Within a month it had been decided to locate the school in Woodstock on property provided by a Baptist deacon, Archibald Burtch.[49] The school became a reality in 1860 when, with *Sit lux* ("Let there be light") as its motto, it formally opened with seventy-nine students, five teachers, and Fyfe as the school's first principal. The school was

---

[46] George W. Campbell, "Canada Baptist College, 1838-1849: The Generation and Demise of a Pioneering Dream in Canadian Theological Education" (MTh thesis, Knox College, 1974).

[47] "Call for an Educational Convention," The Christian Messenger, 3, no.4 (October 23, 1856): 2, cols. 3-4.

[48] "What was done at the Convention?," *The Christian Messenger*, 3, no.9 (November 27, 1856): 2, cols. 2-3 and "Baptist Educational Convention," *The Christian Messenger*, 3, no.9 (November 27, 1856): 2, cols. 7-8.

[49] "R. A. Fyfe, W. Wilkinson, and Hoyes Lloyd, "Location of the Baptist Institute," *The Christian Messenger*, 3, no.13 (December 25, 1856): 2, col. 7.

enormously influential in giving shape and cohesion to the Baptist cause in Ontario—some of its key leaders in the last forty years of the nineteenth century came from the school, including pastors like E. W. Dadson (1845-1900) and the first overseas missionaries of the Ontario Baptist community, John McLaurin (1839-1912) and Americus Vespucius Timpany (1840-1885).

The year following Fyfe's death in 1878, the multi-millionaire Baptist entrepreneur William McMaster (1811-1887)—whose assets in 1859 were estimated at \$600,000-\$800,000[50]—persuaded his fellow Baptists at a special educational convention that was held at First Baptist, Guelph, to accept his offer of funding the move of the theological wing of the Canadian Literary Institute to Toronto. As Daniel Edmund Thomson (1851-?), a fellow member of Jarvis Street Baptist Church and prominent Toronto lawyer, observed, McMaster was convinced that the Baptists were "a people of destiny" and he remained in that denomination even though his "business and social welfare would have been greatly promoted by his union with one of the larger and stronger bodies."[51] A year later, McMaster had found and purchased a site for the school on Bloor Street, then the northern border of Toronto. He gave an initial outlay of \$100,000 to erect the building for the school and promised to give an annual contribution of approximately \$14,000. He was quite reluctant to have his name associated with the building, but his wishes were disregarded and the building was named McMaster Hall. His insistence, however, that the school in Toronto be called a college

---

[50] "McMaster, William," *Dictionary of Canadian Biography* (http://www.biographi.ca/en/bio/mcmaster_william_11E.html accessed October 5, 2017).

[51] D. E. Thomson, "William McMaster," *McMaster University Monthly*, 1 (1891-1892): 97-103. Cf. J. M. Cramp's optimistic lecture *The "Future" of the Baptists and Their Duty to Prepare for It* (Halifax, NS, [1852]).

rather than a seminary, an American term, was followed. A possible hope that some arts subjects might be taught to supplement the theological curriculum may account for his insistence in this regard. This explains why the school took the name Toronto Baptist College before it opened its doors to students in the fall of 1881.[52]

"Jesus, Wondrous Saviour"

The second principal of Toronto Baptist College was Daniel Arthur McGregor (1847–1890), whose ministry at the school and a hymn that he wrote shortly before his death reveal the tremendous depth of Ontarian Evangelical piety. McGregor was born in the Ottawa Valley to Scottish emigrants Alexander and Clementine McGregor, who were converted during a long-remembered revival in the Ottawa Valley in the mid-1830s.[53] Daniel was the younger of twins and the fifth child of the family. He grew up in a rural environment where he had virtually no opportunities for formal schooling after the age of 12. But he had a keen interest in reading, which did him in good stead during these formative years.

Led to Christ in June, 1867 by his eldest brother Malcolm, he joined the Osgoode Baptist Church, which had been pastored by Daniel McPhail (1811–1874), the "Elijah of the Ottawa Valley." The Osgoode work was a remarkable Church, known far and wide for its piety and knowledge of the Scriptures. As McGregor's contemporary E. W. Dadson put it: "There was no escaping God and the Bible in that community."[54] It is no

---

[52] "McMaster, William."
[53] *Memoir of Daniel Arthur McGregor* (2nd ed.; Toronto, ON: The Alumni Association of Toronto Baptist College, 1891), 12–14.
[54] *Memoir of Daniel Arthur McGregor*, 24.

surprise that McGregor "was familiar with deep theological questions from his early youth."[55]

Three years after McGregor's conversion, with the cordial recommendation of his home church in Osgoode, he left for the Canadian Literary Institute in Woodstock, from which he graduated in 1878. Over the next two years he pastored Baptist churches in Whitby and Brooklin, while studying for his B.A. at University of Toronto. He obtained this degree in 1881, the same year that he moved to Stratford to pastor the town's Baptist cause. He was there for five years before accepting an offer from Toronto Baptist College in 1886 to assume the professorship in homiletics. Two years later he was asked to teach apologetics and systematic theology instead.

Every lecture that he delivered cost him many hours of close study and reflection about how to make it a lesson in practical Christianity. He was convinced that he should never go before his students with anything but the most careful preparation. A former student thus recollected his teaching—a recollection that reveals the way that nineteenth-century Evangelical piety was a deeply affective faith:

> He not only thought out the... doctrines upon which he lectured, but he felt their power, and falling tears often evinced his emotion while he spoke of some particular aspect of the truth. This made us all feel that we had before us not only a theological professor but also a Christian man whose life was swayed by the great principles about which he spoke. I find it hard to estimate the value of such a view of Christian doctrines. He must be a brilliant botanist who can not only give to his students a strictly accurate knowledge of flowers, but can also inspire in them an enthusiastic

---

[55] *Memoir of Daniel Arthur McGregor*, 26.

admiration for their aesthetic beauty. This was what Professor McGregor succeeded in doing. He not only made us see the truth, but he made us feel its power and perceive its beauty.[56]

In the spring of 1889, McGregor was chosen to succeed John H. Castle (1830-1890) as Principal of Toronto Baptist College. But McGregor was in office only a year before he succumbed to Pott's disease, a tubercular inflammation of the spinal column. Symptoms of the disease first showed themselves in June of 1889, when McGregor began to complain of a "peculiar pain in his back." By August he was completely paralyzed in the lower half of his body. Eventually, he underwent an operation on his spine in St. Luke's Hospital, New York City, on April 16, 1890, but complications set in and he died on April 25, 1890. His body was brought back to Toronto by his grieving widow, Augusta, and Malcolm, his eldest brother, both of whom had been at his bedside when he died. He was buried in Mount Pleasant Cemetery in Toronto.[57]

During his confinement to his bed during the autumn months of 1889, McGregor composed a hymn that his brother Malcolm would later describe as being "expressive of adoring love and ardent longing for the Saviour."[58] William H. Brackney has well described this hymn as a "striking Christological" contribution to Canadian evangelical piety.[59] In time this hymn, "Jesus, Wondrous Saviour," became known as the McMaster Hymn and has been often sung at official McMaster University events.

---

[56] *Memoir of Daniel Arthur McGregor*, 80-81.
[57] *Memoir of Daniel Arthur McGregor*, 94-122.
[58] *Memoir of Daniel Arthur McGregor*, 101.
[59] William H. Brackney, "Inside the Canadian Baptist Theological Tradition" (Unpublished lecture, November 12, 1994).

The full hymn runs as follows, though stanzas 2 and 3 are usually omitted today.

> Jesus, wondrous Saviour!
> Christ, of kings the King![60]
> Angels fall before Thee
> Prostrate, worshipping.[61]
> Fairest they confess Thee
> In the Heavens above,
> We would sing Thee fairest
> Here in hymns of love.
>
> Fairer far than sunlight
> Unto eyes that wait
> Amid fear and darkness
> Till the morning break;
> Fairer than the day-dawn,
> Hills and dates among,
> When its tide of glory
> Wakes the tide of song.
> Sweeter far than music
> Quivering from keys
> That unbind all feeling
> With strange harmonies.
> Thou art more and dearer
> Than all minstrelsy;
> Only in Thy presence
> Can joy's fulness be.[62]
>
> All earth's flowing pleasures
> Were a wintry sea;
> Heaven itself without Thee
> Dark as night would be.

---

[60] Revelation 17:14; 19:16.
[61] Revelation 5:14; 7:11; 5:8.
[62] Psalm 16:11.

Lamb of God! Thy glory[63]
Is the light above.
Lamb of God! Thy glory
Is the life of love.

Life is death if severed
From Thy throbbing heart.
Death with life abundant
At Thy touch would start.
Worlds and men and angels
All consist in Thee:[64]
Yet Thou camest to us
In humility.[65]

Jesus! all perfections
Rise and end in Thee;
Brightness of God's glory[66]
Thou, eternally.
Favour'd beyond measure
They Thy face who see;
May we, gracious Saviour,
Share this ecstasy.

This supremely Christ-centred hymn begins and ends with the worship of Christ in heaven. In the first stanza, it is angelic worship that is depicted and urged as a model for human worship in this world. Stanzas 2 and 3 are, in some ways, typical of Victorian sentimentalism, but surely we see in them the comfort that McGregor drew from the person of Christ during the times of "fear and darkness" in hospital in New York City. His hope is an eschatological one, similar to the hope expressed in

---

[63] John 1:29; Revelation 5:6; 21:23.
[64] Colossians 1:17.
[65] Matthew 11:29; Philippians 2:7-8.
[66] Hebrews 1:3.

Hebrews 11:16, with which this essay opened: the enjoyment of Christ in the world to come. These two stanzas build to the climax at the close of the third stanza: "Only in Thy presence/Can joy's fulness be."

The fourth stanza takes its rise from this conclusion—a good reason for not omitting stanza 3 or stanza 2. Compared to the joy of being in Christ's actual presence, all of the pleasures of this world (and McGregor's words in stanzas 2 and 3 clearly indicate that he could enjoy earthly pleasures) are like the perishing cold of a wintry sea. In fact, the hymnist goes on to say, heaven itself would be robbed of its light and glory if Christ were not in it.

The word "life" at the close of the fourth stanza is what is picked up by stanza 5, a profound mini-reflection on death and life. True death precedes physical death for those not joined to Christ and physical death is not really death if the one dying is a Christian. Death and life are thus ultimately not merely physical states, but spiritual ones. And what McGregor finds amazing is that the One who gives the true life that triumphs over death, the One who sustains the entire universe (a clear reference to Colossians 1:17, which had been adopted in 1888 as the motto of Toronto Baptist College and later that of McMaster University), came into this world "in humility" and human frailty. He is obviously thinking here of Philippians 2, and its great hymn to Christ.

The final stanza continues to laud Christ—now in words drawn from Hebrews 1—and ends where the hymn began: in the glory of the heavenly worship of Jesus. In the face of all of his suffering, McGregor has this prayerful hope: to see the face of his "gracious Saviour." This is true "ecstasy," of which the pleasures in this world are pale reflections. Though written by a dying man this hymn is suffused with joy in Christ and the conviction that only in the glory of his presence can he, as a human being, know the height of human pleasure. In the face of death these verses became McGregor's personal affirmation of his faith in a risen, glorified Saviour.

Coming from a product of the Ontario Baptist community and the hand of one who was serving at the time as the principal of his denomination's theological seminary, "Jesus, wondrous savior" well encapsulates the way in which the lives and thought of many of these late nineteenth-century Baptists "desired a better country."[67]

---

[67] This hymn also illustrates the astute comment by American historian Mark Noll that "the religion of the classical evangelical hymns is evangelicalism at its best," for they "contain the clearest, most memorable, the most cohesive, and the most widely repeated expressions of what it means to be an evangelical" (*American Evangelical Christianity: An Introduction* [Oxford, UK/Malden, MA: Blackwell Publishers, 2011], 268).

2
A Century of Change: Protestantism in Canada in the Twentieth Century

Kevin N. Flatt

A Canadian time-traveller from 1900 transported suddenly a century into the future would be struck by many differences between the dawn of the twentieth century and the dawn of the twenty-first. Most immediately obvious would be the changes to material conditions of life in Canada: the ubiquity of the automobile and the disappearance of horses, the greatly increased size and ethnic diversity of the population, the changes in everyday patterns of dress and speech. Given time, however, if our chronologically dislocated observer possessed a keen eye and a wise mind, he or she would also take note of less visible, but equally important, changes in the beliefs and values of Canadians concerning matters of ultimate importance: the existence and character of higher powers, the meaning and purpose of life, and the nature of truth, goodness, and beauty.

One of these less visible but deeply important changes would be the wholesale transformation of the dominant religious faith of English-speaking Canada, Protestantism. While some of the Protestant denominations and even a few of their buildings would be familiar to the time-traveller, much of what went on inside them would seem strange indeed; and our observer would find that on any given Sunday most Protestants would not be worshipping inside them at all, but could either be found engaged in quite secular pursuits, or worshipping at strange and even rather outlandish churches of unknown provenance.

This essay addresses the broad topic of Protestantism in Canada in the twentieth century, focusing on the enormous changes Protestantism underwent in that period. To bring this story into focus, the essay first examines the mainline Protestant churches which once dominated English Canada, and how they underwent a slow-motion collapse over the course of the twentieth century. Next, it turns to the evangelical churches outside the mainline, which went from being fairly small churches on the margins to the new, vital core of Canadian Protestantism. Finally, the essay asks what all of this has meant for the character of the country as a whole.

The argument, in brief, is that while the mainline churches largely abandoned their heritage and thus their role as the standard-bearer for the gospel in Canada, the newer evangelical churches took up that standard and became the new core of Protestantism in this country. Nevertheless, the new evangelical core did not enjoy as wide a reach as its predecessors. Canada as a whole still lost some things in the transition, and the new role of the evangelical churches also came with new temptations, and new dangers. What was at stake in these changes was nothing less than whether there would continue to be a faithful voice for the gospel—and the faith once delivered to the saints—in this northern dominion.

Mainline Protestantism

Mainline Protestantism includes the three denominations which held the allegiance of the large majority of Protestants in the first half of the twentieth century. In order of size, they were, first, the United Church of Canada, which was established in 1925 by a merger of the Methodist and Congregationalist denominations and about two-thirds of the Presbyterian churches; second, the Anglican Church of Canada, formerly the Church of England in Canada; and third, the Presbyterian Church in Canada, sometimes known after 1925 as the "continuing Presbyterians" because they were the ones who stayed out of the union that formed the United Church.

Early in the century, the Methodist/United, Anglican, and Presbyterian churches dominated the religious scene in the English-speaking parts of the country. In the 1931 census, for example, 44% of the Canadian population claimed to belong to one of these three churches, meaning that they commanded the allegiance of an impressive 82% of all Protestants in Canada. Four decades later, in the 1971 census, nearly four out of five Protestants still indicated Anglican, Presbyterian, or United as their denomination.[1] "Mainline" is therefore a fitting label for these churches in the twentieth century. To get a sense of the massive changes that these churches experienced over the course of the century, it is helpful to think in terms of three major transitions.

From Evangelical Heritage to Liberal Experiment
In the nineteenth century all three of these denominations (including here the precursors to the United Church) had largely been committed to an evangelical inheritance that combined three layers: historic, orthodox Christianity; the core convictions of the Protestant Reformation; and the values of the evangelical revivals of the eighteenth century, such as the importance

---

[1] Statistics Canada, *Historical Statistics of Canada*, 2nd ed. (1999), table A164–184. http://www.statcan.gc.ca/pub/11-516-x/se ctiona/4147436-eng.htm#1 (accessed July 24, 2017).

of a living personal faith in Jesus Christ and the urgent need to spread the gospel to all those who did not possess saving faith.[2]

What happened over the course of the twentieth century is that all three layers of this evangelical faith were exchanged by the mainline Protestant churches for something called liberalism or modernism. Liberalism either denied the central doctrines of evangelical faith or redefined them to bear new meanings. In place of Scriptures that were God-breathed and therefore authoritative, liberals believed in a Bible that merely recorded the fallible religious ideas of primitive men. In place of a virgin-born, miracle-performing, crucified and resurrected Jesus, they believed in a Jesus who was conceived in the ordinary way, who provided merely psychological healing, and who had only risen from the dead in a metaphorical sense.

Thus, liberalism was not just a denial of this or that evangelical doctrine, but an entirely different worldview from evangelical Christianity. Evangelical scholar J. Gresham Machen famously argued that liberalism was not really Christianity at all, but a *different religion* that happened to be using much of the same terminology.[3]

This rival religion of liberalism found its way into Canadian seminaries and pulpits in the later nineteenth century, due to

---

[2] On the evangelical character of much of nineteenth-century Protestantism in Canada, see Michael Haykin's essay in this volume. The three-layer definition of evangelicalism is elaborated and defended in Kevin N. Flatt, *After Evangelicalism: The Sixties and the United Church of Canada* (Montreal & Kingston: McGill-Queen's University Press, 2013), 7-10.

[3] J. Gresham Machen, *Christianity and Liberalism* (Grand Rapids, MI: Eerdmans, 1946 [1923]). See also the same point from a liberal perspective in a 1924 editorial in the *Christian Century*, quoted in Robert K. Burkinshaw, *Pilgrims in Lotus Land: Conservative Protestantism in British Columbia, 1917-1981* (Montreal & Kingston: McGill-Queen's University Press, 1995), 12.

various factors: immense cultural pressures among the highly educated, the duplicity of professors and pastors who claimed to assent to creeds and confessions they actually denied, and the complacency of church leaders who failed to combat the inroads of the new theology.[4] By the time of World War I liberalism had captured the governing structures of the Methodist and Presbyterian churches, and, to a lesser degree, of the Anglican church as well.

The transition from evangelicalism to liberalism was a top-down process that took many decades to play out. The older evangelical faith continued to live in the hearts of many clergy into the middle part of the twentieth century, and in the hearts of many laypeople for a couple of decades beyond that.[5] Many

---

[4] On the rise of liberalism in Canadian Protestantism, see D. C. Masters, "The Rise of Liberalism in Canadian Protestant Churches," *CCHA Study Sessions*, 36 (1969), 27–39; and for the broader context, see Ramsey Cook, *The Regenerators: Social Criticism in Late Victorian English Canada* (Toronto: University of Toronto Press, 1985); Michael Gauvreau, *The Evangelical Century: College and Creed in English Canada from the Great Revival to the Great Depression* (Montreal & Kingston: McGill-Queen's University Press, 1991); and David Marshall, *Secularizing the Faith: Canadian Protestant Clergy and the Crisis of Belief, 1850–1940* (Toronto: University of Toronto Press, 1992).

[5] Several historians suggest the continuing strength of evangelicalism in some mainline Protestant circles through the middle part of the century. See Nancy Christie and Michael Gauvreau, *A Full-Orbed Christianity: The Protestant Churches and Social Welfare in Canada, 1900–1940* (Montreal & Kingston: McGill-Queen's University Press, 1996); David Plaxton, "'We Will Evangelize with a Whole Gospel or None:' Evangelicalism and the United Church of Canada," in *Aspects of the Canadian Evangelical Experience*, edited by George A. Rawlyk (Montreal & Kingston: McGill-Queen's University Press, 1997); William Katerberg, "Redefining Evangelicalism in the Canadian Anglican Church: Wycliffe College and the Evangelical Party, 1867–1995," in Rawlyk, ed., *Aspects of the Canadian Evangelical Experience*; and Barry Mack, "From Preaching to Propaganda to Marginalization: The Lost

of the theological changes took place gradually and behind the scenes, such that only people in high leadership positions were fully aware of what was going on. While this was happening, there were outward signs well into the middle of the century that evangelicalism was alive and well in the mainline. The United Church, for example, continued to pour time and money into mass evangelism campaigns in the 1930s, 1940s, and 1950s, complete with altar calls challenging people to commit their lives to Christ.[6] Indeed, as late as the 1950s the American evangelical Billy Graham's evangelistic crusades in Canada received widespread support from United ministers and local bodies, even though some church leaders and commentators expressed reservations about aspects of his theology.[7] Not very many people thought to ask what theology, exactly, United Church leaders thought lay behind their use of phrases like "commit one's life to Christ," but it all looked very much like the old evangelicalism, and it was still *just* possible to feel at home as an evangelical in the United Church if you did not look too closely at the things being taught in the colleges or in the publications from church headquarters.

This process also happened, though more slowly and less thoroughly, in the other two mainline denominations. The Anglican attachment to tradition helped impede the impact of liberalism for a while, and the Presbyterians who rejected union in 1925 tended to have a more conservative temperament than those who joined the United Church.[8] In the end, however,

---

Centre of Twentieth-Century Presbyterianism" in Rawlyk, ed., *Aspects of the Canadian Evangelical Experience*.

[6] Flatt, *After Evangelicalism*, chaps. 1-2.

[7] Flatt, *After Evangelicalism*, 68-69.

[8] Ian S. Rennie, "Conservatism in the Presbyterian Church in Canada in 1925 and Beyond: An Introductory Explanation," paper

liberalism exercised great influence among Canada's Anglicans as well, especially after World War II. For all three churches the 1960s were the crucial decade. In those years liberalism assumed a position of open dominance in the United and Anglican churches, and even made its influence felt among the Presbyterians.[9] In this limited space it is impossible to do justice to the full extent of the religious turmoil of "the Sixties," but it is worth considering some of the main developments.

First, a new, more virulent strain of liberal theology emerged internationally, associated with names like Paul Tillich (1886-1965), Rudolf Bultmann (1884-1976), John A.T. Robinson (1919-1983), and the "death of God" movement. It received a warm welcome from United and Anglican leaders in Canada.[10] The Anglican establishment, for example, commissioned the prominent journalist Pierre Berton (1920-2004) to write a book criticizing the Protestant churches as frankly as possible. To put him on the right track, Ernest Harrison, an official at the Anglican Department of Religious Education, gave Berton a copy of radical theologian Bishop Robinson's book *Honest to God* for inspiration. As Harrison no doubt hoped, Berton's book *The Comfortable Pew*, which became a runaway bestseller by Canadian standards, drew heavily on Robinson's ideas in

---

presented to the Canadian Society of Presbyterian History (1982), 43. http://www.csph.ca/assets/1982-rennie.pdf (accessed July 27, 2017).

[9] Although it is not directly addressed by his essay, this trend can be seen among Anglicans in William H. Katerberg, "Redefining Evangelicalism in the Canadian Anglican Church: Wycliffe College and the Evangelical Party, 1867-1995," in Rawlyk, ed., *Aspects of the Canadian Evangelical Experience*. A perusal of the pages of the official Anglican publication, the *Canadian Churchman*, particularly in the 1960s, readily illustrates this shift. On Presbyterians, see Mack, "From Preaching to Propaganda to Marginalization," 149-153.

[10] Flatt, *After Evangelicalism*, 152-162.

castigating the churches for their outmoded attachment to "dogma" and "mythological" beliefs.[11] (Not to be outdone in self-criticism, the United Church produced its own volume of critical essays the following year, including a piece by Berton.)[12]

Liberal theology was nothing new, but these developments went further than previous waves of liberal thought, and played out much more publicly. The United Church, for example, broke with tradition and created a Sunday school curriculum with the explicit aim of undermining belief in the literal truth of the Bible.[13] In July 1964, Canadians were startled by headlines in the major newspapers revealing that the curriculum questioned the historical reality of the virgin birth, the creation account, Noah's ark, the Israelite crossing of the Red Sea, and even the bodily resurrection of Jesus.[14] In keeping with its skepticism about the supernatural, the curriculum somehow managed to retell the account of the temptation of Jesus in the wilderness without once mentioning the devil—not an easy thing to do![15] Liberal theology thus became inescapable for ordinary United Church

---

[11] Pierre Berton, *The Comfortable Pew* (Toronto: McClelland and Stewart, 1965). For the origins, sales, and reception of the book, see Flatt, *After Evangelicalism*, 162–165.

[12] United Church of Canada, Board of Evangelism and Social Service, *Why the Sea is Boiling Hot* (Toronto: Board of Evangelism and Social Service, 1965). For context, see Flatt, *After Evangelicalism*, 196.

[13] On the curriculum, see the overview in Kevin N. Flatt, "The 'New Curriculum' Controversy and the Religious Crisis of the United Church of Canada, 1952-1965," in *The Sixties and Beyond: Dechristianization in North America and Western Europe, 1945-2000*, edited by Nancy Christie and Michael Gauvreau (Toronto: University of Toronto Press, 2012), and the more detailed account in Flatt, *After Evangelicalism*, chaps. 3–4.

[14] Allen Spraggett, "Virgin Birth, Goliath—Are They Just Myths?" *Toronto Daily Star*, 4 July 1964, 1.

[15] Flatt, *After Evangelicalism*, 114.

members and their children—unless, of course, they left the church (more on that below).

Meanwhile, the churches also softened or reversed their positions on matters of morality. Without feeling obliged to follow the Bible, the creeds, the confessions, or the tradition of the church, they had no good reason to resist the pull of the Sexual Revolution that was beginning to take hold in Canada. Increasingly, United Church leaders and clergy gave up on the idea that sex was only permitted within marriage; one director of pastoral counselling in the Toronto area, Mervyn Dickinson, was even quoted in the press to say that an extramarital affair could be "a beautiful and constructive relationship."[16]

The United Church's official bodies not only dropped their moral opposition to abortion, but under the leadership of J. R. Hord (1919-1968), secretary of their Board of Evangelism and Social Service, they strenuously lobbied the government to make it widely legally available.[17] The impact of these changes on the United Church, the most liberal of the three denominations, can perhaps be summed up by this observation: the church that had enthusiastically supported Billy Graham and strenuously criticized abortion in the 1950s, by the end of the 1960s enthusiastically supported abortion and strenuously criticized Billy Graham.[18] Many Anglicans were not far behind, and although the Presbyterians did not move nearly as quickly or as far to the left as the other mainline churches, the pages of the *Presbyterian Record* in these years show the influence of similar pressures.[19]

---

[16] Flatt, *After Evangelicalism*, 218-219.

[17] Flatt, *After Evangelicalism*, 220-221.

[18] On opposition to and controversy about Graham in the United Church in the 1960s, see Flatt, *After Evangelicalism*, 205-215.

[19] For a few examples of such trends in Anglicanism in this period see, "Sex, Sex, Sex," *Canadian Churchman*, February 1965, 4; Arnold Edinborough, "With Charity for All," *Canadian Churchman*,

The 1960s set the tone, in fact, for the rest of the century. Although there were important new developments, such as the gradual acceptance of homosexuality in first the United and then the Anglican churches, these developments followed the same trajectory that had been set in the Sixties. Despite resistance in some quarters, especially among conservative Presbyterians and Anglicans who could look to their more orthodox counterparts in other countries, mainline Protestantism as a whole in Canada exchanged evangelicalism for liberalism.

From Mainline to Sideline

In all three mainline Protestant churches, theological liberalization was followed by numerical decline and social irrelevance. As mentioned above, in 1931 four out of five Protestants in Canada, and close to half of the population as a whole, identified with the United, Anglican, or Presbyterian churches. With their services, Sunday schools, and revival and temperance and educational

---

September 1965, 4; "C. of E. Reports: Some Abortions May be Justified," *Canadian Churchman*, March 1966, 12; "Why Not Ordain Women?" *Canadian Churchman*, May 1971, 4; "Synod Avoids Taking Abortion Stand," *Canadian Churchman*, March 1971, 27. For the influence of the Sexual Revolution among Presbyterians, see "Divorce and Birth Control," *Presbyterian Record*, March 1965, 4; Wayne A. Smith, "Should Canada Prohibit Abortion?" *Presbyterian Record*, 14-5; Valerie M. Dunn, "Women's Comfortable Cocoons," *Presbyterian Record*, October 1970, 4. Nevertheless, the Presbyterians remained closer to the evangelical churches in this regard, and others, than did the other mainline denominations. It is telling that there were more Presbyterian students than United and Anglican students combined at the evangelical Toronto Bible College in 1967. John G. Stackhouse, Jr., *Canadian Evangelicalism in the Twentieth Century: An Introduction to Its Character* (Toronto: University of Toronto Press, 1993), 68. More general changes among Presbyterians in the 1960s and subsequently are also addressed briefly in Mack, "From Preaching to Propaganda to Marginalization," 151-152.

campaigns, they had the character of a mass movement, playing an important, even a central, role in the formation of the values of English Canadian society.

Over the following decades, however, the influence and size of these churches dwindled. The decline began in the 1960s, when all three denominations reached their peak number of members and began to lose more people than they were adding. Over the remainder of the century, each denomination lost about 40% of their members—during a period of time in which the Canadian population as a whole *increased* by 53%. Thus, by the 2001 census, only about one in six Canadians told census-takers that they belonged to one of these churches (compared, again, to nearly 3 in 6 back in 1931).[20] This amounted to a huge loss in market share. As striking as these figures are, they mask the true extent of the decline, because people continued to *call* themselves Anglican or United on the census long after they stopped actually *attending* church and gave up their membership. For example, of the 2.8 million Canadians who told the 2001 census-takers that they belonged to the United Church, less than a quarter were actually members of the United Church, and only a

---

[20] For denominational membership figures, see United Church of Canada, *Yearbook*; Anglican Church of Canada, *Yearbook*, *General Synod Journal*, and documents provided by the General Synod Archives, Toronto (my thanks to Laurel Parsons for assistance in obtaining these documents); Presbyterian Church in Canada, *Acts and Proceedings of the General Assembly*. For 2001 census data, see Statistics Canada, "Selected Religions, for Canada, Provinces and Territories: 20% Sample Data," *2001 Census* (Ottawa) www12.statcan.ca/english/census01/products/highlight/Religion/Page.cfm?Lang=E&Geo=PR&View=1a&Code=01&Table=1&StartRec=1&Sort=2&B1=Canada&B2=1 (accessed July 27, 2017).

tenth attended worship on an average Sunday.[21] On top of this, by the end of the century, mainline Protestants gave much less money per capita and volunteered less for church causes than adherents of evangelical or conservative Protestant churches.[22] In short, their remaining support was thin and getting thinner.

With a decline in numbers and funds comes, of course, a decline in social influence. Already in the 1981 debate about whether to include a reference to God in the preamble to the new Charter of Rights and Freedoms, then Prime Minister Pierre Elliott Trudeau compared the numbers of mainline Protestants training for pastoral ministry with the number of evangelical Protestants doing the same. He concluded that he should listen to the evangelicals, not the mainliners, because the future belonged to the former.[23] The mainline had become the sideline.

From Establishment Conscience to Progressive Acolytes
The third transition was mainline Protestantism's changing role in Canadian society, from attempting to serve as the conscience of the establishment, to becoming acolytes of progressive activists. Through the first half of the twentieth century, in the English-speaking parts of the country, mainline Protestantism was

---

[21] Compare the 2001 census affiliation figure for the United Church (2, 839, 125) with the official denominational figures for membership (651, 002) and average weekly attendance (270, 361).

[22] Reginald Bibby, *Unknown Gods: The Ongoing Story of Religion in Canada* (Toronto: Stoddart, 1993), 108; Kurt Bowen, *Christians in a Secular World: The Canadian Experience* (Montreal & Kingston: McGill-Queen's University Press, 2004) 158, 166, 175.

[23] George Egerton, "Trudeau, God, and the Canadian Constitution: Religion, Human Rights, and Government Authority in the Making of the 1982 Constitution," in *Rethinking Church, State and Modernity: Canada between Europe and America*, edited by David Lyon and Marguerite Van Die (Toronto: University of Toronto Press, 2000), 104–106, esp. note 24.

interwoven with most social institutions. Public schools at that time were in effect mainline Protestant schools, with an ethos and religious curriculum that reflected mainline Protestant preferences.[24] The leading English-speaking universities had been founded by mainline Protestant churches, and both denominationally controlled and non-denominational universities were dominated by what Catherine Gidney calls a "liberal Protestant establishment."[25] Protestant politicians tended to belong to one of these churches—all of Canada's prime ministers in the first half of the century, for example, apart from Sir Wilfrid Laurier and Louis St. Laurent, who were Catholics, were affiliated, however loosely, with the Anglican, Presbyterian, or United churches. Social life, especially in small towns and rural areas, tended to centre on the mainline Protestant church halls.

Moreover, the United Church at least, as the largest Protestant denomination, saw itself as the guardian of society's moral values. In the words of W. J. Gallagher (1894–1964), chairman of the church's Board of Evangelism and Social Service in the late 1930s, the church was a "colony of heaven," with a mandate to exercise a heavenly influence throughout Canadian society and its institutions.[26] This included a self-appointed role

---

[24] R. D. Gidney and W. P. J. Millar, "The Christian Recessional in Ontario's Public Schools," in *Religion and Public Life in Canada: Historical and Comparative Perspectives*, edited by Marguerite Van Die (Toronto: University of Toronto Press, 2001).

[25] Catherine Gidney, *A Long Eclipse: The Liberal Protestant Establishment and the Canadian University, 1920–1970* (Montreal & Kingston: McGill-Queen's University Press, 2004).

[26] Flatt, *After Evangelicalism*, 33. More generally, on the United Church's guiding vision to build a certain kind of Christian Canada, from the church's founding to the 1960s, see Phyllis Airhart, *A Church with the Soul of a Nation: Making and Remaking the United Church of Canada* (Montreal & Kingston: McGill-Queen's University Press, 2014).

as a moral authority and watchdog. The United Church regularly provided advice—usually unsolicited advice—to federal and provincial and city governments about the kinds of laws and policies that would make for a more upright country.

This role of the mainline churches as a conscience of the establishment collapsed in the 1960s and the following decades, for several reasons. One reason was the numerical decline discussed earlier, which undercut the credibility of the churches when speaking in the public square, and eventually sapped their resources. Another reason was the increasing secularization of public institutions after the 1950s—including the universities, government, and eventually the public schools.[27] By the last third of the century, the establishment institutions no longer belonged to the mainline Protestant churches.

But another reason that the mainline churches lost their role as a "colony of heaven" is that they stopped believing that they *should* play that role. Instead, a new generation of mainline leaders in the 1960s saw the church as part of the *problem* and took their cues instead from radical progressive movements led by secular activists. The main role of the church in society, as they saw it, was to get out of the way, to get on board with where society was going, and to apologize for having taken so long to do so. This was the main argument of Berton's *Comfortable Pew*, as

---

[27] On universities, see Gidney, *A Long Eclipse*; on public schools in Ontario, see Gidney and Millar, "The Christian Recessional." For an overview of the increasingly secular tone of government in this period, see Mark A. Noll, "What Happened to Christian Canada?" *Church History* 75 no. 2 (June 2006): 245-273; see also the fascinating overview of the debate over the inclusion of a reference to God in the 1982 constitution in George Egerton, "Trudeau, God, and the Canadian Constitution: Religion, Human Rights and Government Authority in the Making of the 1982 Constitution," in Van Die, ed., *Rethinking Church, State, and Modernity*.

Harrison and his colleagues had hoped.[28] On issue after issue, the mainline churches adopted progressive political and social causes, most tellingly in the area of gender and sexuality.[29] Indeed, the agencies of these churches often found themselves "ahead of the curve" on causes like feminism, abortion, and gay marriage. In a play on the old British joke that the Church of England was "the Tory party at prayer," some Canadian quipped that the United Church had become "the NDP at prayer."[30]

Thus, the mainline churches that began the century trying to act as the conscience of the establishment, as *leaders* of opinion, ended the century as devoted *followers* of the secular Zeitgeist, cheering along left-wing and progressive movements—but from a largely irrelevant position on the sidelines.

Evangelicalism Outside the Mainline

Having discussed the changes in the mainline Protestant churches, we will now turn our attention to the remaining evangelical churches—that is, groups outside of the mainline churches that still adhered to historical Christian orthodoxy, the core claims of the Reformation, and an evangelical emphasis on a living personal relationship with Christ.

Who were these evangelicals? As Bob Burkinshaw notes in his book *Pilgrims in Lotus Land*, an excellent study of conservative Protestantism in British Columbia, in the twentieth century

---

[28] Flatt, *After Evangelicalism*, 193–196.

[29] For the United Church, see Flatt, *After Evangelicalism*, chap. 6.

[30] I have been unable to identify the original source of this now-proverbial saying. For an example of its recent use in Canadian news media, see Margaret Wente, "The Collapse of the Liberal Church," *Globe and Mail*, July 28, 2012. beta.theglobeandmail.com/globe-debate/the-collapse-of-the-liberal-church/article4443228/(accessed October 19, 2017).

the backbone of the Canadian evangelical movement outside of the mainline denominations was made up of two groups: Baptists and Pentecostals.[31] The Baptists were the oldest and most well-established of the continuing evangelical groups in Canada, so much so that in certain times and places some Baptists could be considered part of the mainline; but there were always enough consistently and even militantly *evangelical* Baptists that it is hard to fit them comfortably into the mainline category. A representative denomination here would be the Fellowship of Evangelical Baptist Churches.[32]

The other part of the Canadian evangelical backbone of the twentieth century was the Pentecostal and charismatic churches. These were actually the newest component of Canadian evangelicalism, having emerged as a distinct group in the early twentieth century, but they enjoyed very rapid growth to the point that their leading denomination, the Pentecostal Assemblies of Canada, became the largest evangelical denomination in Canada by the latter part of the century.[33] The Pentecostals, together with similar charismatic churches, carried forward the piety and much of the theology of John Wesley, early Methodism, and the Holiness movement, with an added emphasis on what they believed were the miraculous gifts of the Holy Spirit, especially speaking in tongues.[34]

---

[31] Burkinshaw, *Pilgrims in Lotus Land*, chaps. 4–5.

[32] Leslie K. Tarr, *This Dominion His Dominion: The Story of Evangelical Baptist Endeavour in Canada* (Willowdale, ON: Fellowship of Evangelical Baptist Churches in Canada, 1968).

[33] Bruce L. Guenther and Outreach Canada, "Denominations in Canada," data obtained from Dr. Guenther.

[34] Thomas William Miller, *Canadian Pentecostals: A History of the Pentecostal Assemblies of Canada*, edited by William A. Griffin (Mississauga, ON: Full Gospel Publishing House, 1994). See also Ronald A.N.

Alongside the Baptists and Pentecostals were several other distinct groups. Two of the more important were certain Mennonite churches, such as the Mennonite Brethren, who had adopted evangelical characteristics often under the influence of Wesleyanism; and certain Dutch Reformed churches, who were theologically orthodox Protestants with evangelical traits going back to eighteenth-century revivals in the Netherlands.[35] The Christian Reformed Church is a good example of this latter group. There were also several evangelical churches that did not belong to one of these four denominational families, such as the Christian and Missionary Alliance.[36]

Considered as a whole, these non-mainline evangelicals also went through three major transformations over the course of the twentieth century, as follows.[37]

Kydd, "Canadian Pentecostalism and the Evangelical Impulse," in Rawlyk, ed., *Aspects of the Canadian Evangelical Experience*.

[35] On Mennonites and evangelicalism, see Bruce L. Guenther, "Living with the Virus: The Enigma of Evangelicalism among Mennonites in Canada," in Rawlyk, ed., *Aspects of the Canadian Evangelical Experience*. To my knowledge, there are no overviews of the history of the Christian Reformed and other Dutch Reformed churches in Canada, but see Jan Veenhof, "A History of Theology and Spirituality in the Dutch Reformed Churches (*Gereformeerde Gementen*), 1892-1992," *Calvin Theological Journal* 28, no. 2 (November 1993).

[36] On the CMA, see Darrel R. Reid, "Towards a Fourfold Gospel: A. B. Simpson, John Salmon, and the Christian and Missionary Alliance in Canada," in Rawlyk, ed., *Aspects of the Canadian Evangelical Experience*.

[37] In identifying these trends, I am drawing on the interpretations of others, especially Burkinshaw, *Pilgrims in Lotus Land*, and two works by John G. Stackhouse, Jr., *Canadian Evangelicalism in the Twentieth Century*, and "The Protestant Experience in Canada since 1945," in *The Canadian Protestant Experience, 1760-1990*, edited by George A. Rawlyk (Montreal & Kingston: McGill-Queen's University Press, 1990).

From Separate Streams to Overlapping Consensus

Obviously there were substantial theological and other differences between these various groups. Some of them held to an Arminian understanding of salvation, others to a Reformed or Calvinist understanding. Some practiced believer's baptism, others infant baptism. Some believed that the "sign gifts" like healing and tongues were still active today, while others believed they had ceased earlier in church history. There were also important cultural differences: both the Mennonites and the Reformed churches, for example, tended to be set apart by the experience of immigration and ethnic distinctiveness.

On an everyday level, perhaps even more important than these theological and cultural differences were differing rules about personal behaviour that functioned as shibboleths to tell who was "in" and who was "out." A useful thought experiment is to imagine a Sunday somewhere in Toronto around 1955.[38] There is a Fellowship Baptist church a few blocks down the road from a Christian Reformed Church, and both of them have just finished their services and the people are milling about. Some Baptist families have piled into their cars, and coming down the street, they pass the CRC church. What do they see on the front steps? A group of men have just come out of the church and they are now lighting up their cigarettes. One can imagine the Baptists thinking, "You know, those Reformed folks seem like decent people but they really have a problem with smoking. They'll probably have a beer with lunch later, too." The Reformed folks,

---

[38] What follows is admittedly speculative, though it does reflect the higher emphasis on such rules governing personal behaviour in evangelical groups prior to the last third of the century. See, for example, the various examples of rules concerning alcohol consumption and courtship at evangelical Bible colleges and their gradual relaxation later in the century mentioned in Stackhouse, *Canadian Evangelicalism in the Twentieth Century*.

for their part, watch the Baptists drive by, go further down the street—and then pull into the parking lot of the newly opened Swiss Chalet restaurant.[39] One can imagine the Reformed folks thinking, "You know, those Baptists seem like decent people but they really have a problem with violating the Sabbath. I've even heard that they only have two services on Sundays instead of three." The serious point to this hypothetical scenario is that as late as the 1950s, there could still be a certain amount of distance and even, at times, suspicion, between different evangelical denominations, based on these kinds of boundary-markers.

Over time, however, this sense of distance was replaced with a growing recognition of what Baptists, Pentecostals, evangelical Mennonites, Reformed Christians, and other evangelicals had in common. Although there were multiple reasons for this change, the main reason was what was happening *outside* of evangelicalism. As we have seen, beginning in the 1960s, mainline Protestantism rapidly began to collapse doctrinally and numerically, and, around the same time, something similar happened to Catholicism, especially in Quebec.[40] Canadian culture in general rapidly secularized from the 1960s onward, resulting in a more

---

[39] According to various online sources, the first Swiss Chalet restaurant opened in Toronto in 1954 on the corner of Bedford Road and Bloor Street West. See Doug Taylor, "History of Toronto's Swiss Chalet," Historic Toronto, https://tayloronhistory.com/2016/10/28/history-of-torontos-swiss-chalet/ (accessed October 31, 2017).

[40] On the religious aspects of Quebec's "Quiet Revolution," see Gregory Baum, "Catholicism and Secularization in Quebec," *Cross Currents* 36 no. 4 (Winter 1986-1987); Michael Gauvreau, "From Rechristianization to Contestation: Catholic Values and Quebec Society, 1931-1970," *Church History* 69 no. 4 (Dec. 2000); and David Seljak, "Why the Quiet Revolution was 'Quiet': The Catholic Church's Reaction to the Secularization of Nationalism in Quebec after 1960," *Canadian Catholic Historical Association Historical Studies* 62 (1996), 109-124.

materialistic and hedonistic society less friendly to orthodox Christianity, especially in the area of sexual morality.[41] In light of these changes, the differences *between* evangelical groups began to seem relatively insignificant. In the 1930s, say, one could look around and most Canadians paid at least lip service to the importance of God and the Bible and Jesus Christ and Christian morality. Not so in the 1970s. If a Baptist looked around in the 1970s and asked, who is still willing to take a stand for belief in God, in the authority of the Bible, in the Lordship of Jesus Christ, and in the sanctity of marriage, who would he notice but Pentecostals and charismatics, Mennonite Brethren, and Christian Reformed folks?[42]

An important marker of this growing sense of evangelical solidarity was the foundation of the Evangelical Fellowship of Canada (EFC) in 1964. Starting with the persistent work of Pentecostal pastor Harry Faught who tried to promote cooperation among evangelical pastors in Toronto, the EFC gradually grew to include most evangelical denominations by the end of the century.[43] Now, there continued to be important differences between evangelicals, and in some groups, particularly in the Mennonite and Reformed world, many people still did not think of

---

[41] A good introduction to the changing relationship between Christianity and Canadian identity in the 1960s is Gary Miedema, *For Canada's Sake: Public Religion, Centennial Celebrations, and the Re-making of Canada in the 1960s* (Montreal & Kingston: McGill-Queen's University Press, 2005). For an interpretation, see Mark Noll, "What Happened to Christian Canada?" *Church History* 75 no. 2 (June 2006): 245–273.

[42] Burkinshaw, *Pilgrims in Lotus Land*, 263–265.

[43] Stackhouse, *Canadian Evangelicalism in the Twentieth Century*, chap. 12. It is worth noting that the EFC also involved substantial participation by mainline evangelicals, especially Presbyterians, at least in its early years. See Stackhouse, *Canadian Evangelicalism*, 166.

themselves as part of a larger evangelical movement.⁴⁴ Nevertheless, by the end of the century, there was a greater sense of shared evangelical identity based on an overlapping consensus around core convictions, and a wider gulf between evangelicals and mainstream society.

From Protestant Fringe to Protestant Centre
Early in the century, non-mainline evangelicals were on the fringes of Protestantism, numerically and in terms of their relation to the larger society.⁴⁵ Adherents of evangelical churches were vastly outnumbered by adherents of the Anglican, United, and Presbyterian churches. Most evangelical denominations were small and not nearly as well known to the average Canadian as the big mainline churches. In fact, as Rick Hiemstra, director of research at the EFC, has shown, up until 1971 most evangelical groups were small enough and unfamiliar enough to census takers that they were not reported in the census data at all; several small evangelical denominations were reclassified by census takers who assumed they must belong to the United Church!⁴⁶ (This is just one of several reasons why twentieth-century Canadian census data on religion should be used with caution, especially when it comes to counting evangelicals.)

Despite their small size, however, these evangelical groups outside the mainline were extraordinarily active, building churches and Sunday schools and Bible colleges and parachurch ministries of all kinds and descriptions.⁴⁷ An organization called

---

⁴⁴ For Mennonites, see Guenther, "Living with the Virus," in Rawlyk, ed., *Aspects of the Canadian Evangelical Experience*, 224-225.

⁴⁵ See, for example, Burkinshaw, *Pilgrims in Lotus Land*, 8.

⁴⁶ Rick Hiemstra, "Evangelicals and the Canadian Census," *Church & Faith Trends* 1 no. 2 (2008), 12.

⁴⁷ For one regional glimpse into this kind of activity, see D. Bruce Hindmarsh, "The Winnipeg Fundamentalist Network, 1910-1940:

the Canadian Sunday School Mission is a good example of this phenomenon. As a nondenominational ministry run by conservative evangelicals, it provided Sunday school teaching, prayer meetings, and Bible memorization contests for children in rural parts of western Canada who lacked access to evangelical church-based instruction. It was so active that wary United Church officials began collecting information about this troublesome evangelical competitor.[48]

Throughout the century, evangelical groups were growing, keeping up with or even exceeding the rate of growth of the Canadian population as a whole.[49] They continued to grow even after the 1960s when the mainline churches went into decline. To give a few examples, between 1960 and 2000 the membership of the Fellowship of Evangelical Baptist Churches and the Mennonite Brethren more than doubled, while the number of persons

---

The Roots of Transdenominational Evangelicalism in Manitoba and Saskatchewan," in Rawlyk, ed., *Aspects of the Canadian Evangelical Experience*, 303-319.

[48] In the 1941-1942 operating year, for example, the Mission ran 349 summer Bible schools with an enrollment of over 5,000 children, and distributed 35,000 tracts. Flatt, *After Evangelicalism*, 56-57. On the Mission more generally, see Burkinshaw, *Pilgrims in Lotus Land*, 123, 156, 175, 223, and Hindmarsh, "The Winnipeg Fundamentalist Network," 308-310.

[49] Reginald Bibby has argued that "conservative Protestants" (a sociological term roughly corresponding to "evangelicals") merely held their own as a percentage of the population over the course of the century, but it should be noted that he uses census data (which probably understates evangelical growth, especially of the smaller groups; see Hiemstra, "Evangelicals and the Canadian Census") rather than denominational membership and attendance figures. Bibby's figure should therefore probably be seen as a lower bound. Reginald Bibby, *Fragmented Gods: The Poverty and Potential of Religion in Canada* (Toronto: Irwin, 1987), 27-28.

served by the Pentecostal Assemblies of Canada nearly tripled.[50] Growth came from the defection of evangelicals from the mainline churches, from immigration, from higher birthrates and retention of children, and from conversion of the unchurched.[51] Contrary to the predictions of Pierre Berton and other members of the liberal intelligentsia, Christian groups that stuck with their beliefs and refused to join the bandwagon of cultural change could, in fact, survive and even thrive in an increasingly secular Canada.[52]

It is important to note that the growth of evangelical churches was not simply an amassing of nominal adherents. Data from the latter part of the century shows that conservative Protestants had, of all Christian groups, consistently the highest levels of commitment to Christian beliefs, church attendance, giving, and volunteering—and personal moral views that were closest to biblical standards and furthest from the national norm.[53] In other words, evangelical numerical growth was more than skin deep. Because it took place while the mainline Protestants were suffering catastrophic losses, these formerly marginal evangelical groups actually came to surpass them as the largest active component of Canadian Protestantism by the end of the century. As Bob Burkinshaw put it, by the 1980s evangelicals were the "worshiping majority in Protestantism"—in other words, on the typical Sunday there were now more Protestants

---

[50] Flatt, *After Evangelicalism*, 240-241.

[51] Bibby, *Fragmented Gods*, 28-31; Stackhouse, "The Protestant Experience," 232; Burkinshaw, *Pilgrims in Lotus Land*, 265-268.

[52] I am here intentionally echoing the language of Christian Smith, with Michael Emerson, Sally Gallagher, Paul Kennedy, and David Sikkink, *American Evangelicalism: Embattled and Thriving* (Chicago: University of Chicago Press, 1998), 118-119.

[53] See, for example, Bowen, *Christians in a Secular World*, 105, 109, 158, 166, 175, 224, 230, 241; Bibby, *Unknown Gods*, 6, 87.

worshipping in evangelical churches than in mainline ones.[54] By Rick Hiemstra's count, in 2001 the combined Sunday attendance of evangelical churches was about 1.1 million people, compared to only about 700,000 for mainline Protestant churches.[55] The change was so great that some observers questioned whether the label "mainline" even made sense any more: as one United Church historian put it, "the mainstream" had now become "a very small dribble."[56] In any event, non-mainline evangelicalism, which had been on the fringes, was now the vital core of Canadian Protestantism.

From Acknowledged Outsiders to Aspiring Insiders
For most of the century, non-mainline evangelicals in Canada were on the outside looking in. Compared to mainliners, they had practically no influence on the major social institutions, the halls of political power, or the centres of cultural production. Many evangelicals were recent immigrants or from less respectable backgrounds with less money and less education than was typical in mainline circles. Many were defectors from the mainline denominations. All of them knew that they were different from the mainline. Even in the first half of the century, when the liberalization of the mainline churches was less advanced and less apparent, evangelicals outside the mainline saw themselves as different.

Not only did evangelicals outside the mainline see themselves as different, but by and large, they were *content* to be different. They accepted their status as outsiders. They did not

---

[54] Burkinshaw, *Pilgrims in Lotus Land*, chap. 9.

[55] Hiemstra, "Evangelicals and the Canadian Census," Table 5, p. 9.

[56] Bob Stewart, quoted in Burkinshaw, *Pilgrims in Lotus Land*, 200.

expect the approval of the wider society, even though it was nominally Christian to an extent that is difficult to imagine today. They certainly did not expect to be able to shape the dominant values of the country to align with their own. Indeed, they saw benefit in having a degree of separation from the culture and values of the wider society as a guard against worldliness, even in a time before the widespread open rejection of Christianity.[57]

This acceptance of outsider status could be seen in many ways. One was the formation of evangelical parachurch organizations that were intentionally set up as *alternatives* to the mainline Protestant options. A good example is the Canadian Sunday School Mission mentioned earlier. Another indication of evangelicals' awareness and acceptance of their outsider status can be seen in the area of education. Some groups, especially among the Mennonites and Reformed churches, established and funded their own faith-based day schools to educate their children—even at a time when the public schools included prayers and Bible teaching in their curriculum. In the area of higher education, evangelicals established Bible colleges and seminaries as alternatives to the older theological colleges and divinity schools that were being influenced by liberalism.[58] These kinds of decisions involved huge sacrifice, financial and otherwise, from what were still quite small evangelical movements. Just as importantly, they involved a willingness to live with the stigma of being outsiders.

Evangelicals' willingness to be on the outside looking in diminished, however, over the second half of the century. Their growth in size, educational attainment, and financial resources

---

[57] On evangelicalism's marginal character and willingness to stand apart from mainstream society in early twentieth-century Canada, a good summary discussion can be found in Burkinshaw, *Pilgrims in Lotus Land*, 8-9, 12-13.

[58] Stackhouse, *Canadian Evangelicalism*, covers several examples.

gave rise to a new confidence. Their new status as the worshipping majority in Protestantism, coupled with the evaporation of mainline Protestant influence, gave rise to a new sense of responsibility. Theological arguments that evangelicals should care about and become involved in public issues, particularly coming from American thinkers like Carl Henry and Francis Schaeffer, gained a heightened sense of urgency from social and legal changes that began to undermine the sanctity of life, the integrity of marriage, and fundamental religious freedoms. By the 1980s, Canadian evangelicals, both as individuals and through their institutions, including the EFC, were less content to sit on the sidelines in the face of social and political change. Instead of accepting perpetual outsider status, they were applying for membership in responsible society and a seat at the decision-making table.[59]

There was a great deal of merit in this course. It is hard to argue against evangelicals' desire to be a voice for biblical values in a world that was losing its moral compass, to speak up for religious freedom when it was threatened, or more generally to take some responsibility for a society in which they were now the second or third-largest religious grouping.[60] An increased emphasis on public engagement and social responsibility was also the logical extension of the institution-building of previous generations. This trend had culminated in the area of education with the development of Christian universities with a broad

---

[59] This is a major emphasis of Stackhouse, *Canadian Evangelicalism*; see, for example, 173, 201.

[60] Second or third-place status depends on whether one counts by census affiliation or active participation; if the former, then mainline Protestants would still surpass evangelical Protestants in number through the end of the century. Using either standard Roman Catholics were more numerous; see Hiemstra, "Evangelicals and the Canadian Census," Table 5, p. 9.

curriculum, such as Trinity Western University (established in 1962) and Redeemer University College (established in 1982), which needed to obtain accreditation and degree-granting powers.[61] Much of this, it needs to be said again, was good and necessary. But the transformation from contended outsider to applicant for a seat at the table was also fraught with temptations. These are dealt with further below.

Implications and Conclusion
This essay concludes with a look at what these changes, both mainline and evangelical, meant for the state of affairs in Canada at the end of the twentieth century.

Beginning with mainline Protestantism, it is clear on the one hand that its collapse has been a grave loss for the country. In the nineteenth and early twentieth centuries the teaching of the mainline Protestant churches, whether from the pulpit or in the Sunday school or through their various campaigns, did much to maintain a certain kind of moral climate in English Canada, largely rooted in biblical norms. The relatively decent, polite, law-abiding, honest, neighbourly character of English-Canadian culture through much of the twentieth century, often remarked upon by visitors, was "funded" by the moral capital built up by a century or more of mainline Protestant teaching and discipline. Although this culture had its serious historical blemishes—as all human cultures do—and often lacked clarity on crucial gospel issues, it was still a genuine accomplishment.[62] The decline of

---

[61] On Trinity Western, see Stackhouse, *Canadian Evangelicalism*, chap. 10. On Redeemer, see brief early comments in Stackhouse, *Canadian Evangelicalism*, 191, and the account by Redeemer's first president, Henry de Bolster, *Stepping Forward in Faith: Redeemer University College, 1974-1994* (Belleville, ON: Guardian Books, 2001).

[62] As Calvin says, even though the pagan Romans fell short of God's standard, we should not be "so stupid as to maintain that the

mainline Protestantism has therefore probably been a major reason for the moral hollowing-out of English-Canadian culture. Much of our society is now using up this moral capital without replacing it.

Moreover, for all that continued to be good in the ministry of the mainline churches—one thinks especially of their work with the poor and marginalized—from an evangelical perspective, their abandonment of a clearly biblical gospel of salvation in favour of the rival religion of liberalism was a disaster for the faith. Though such statements are deemed at best impolite today, it needs to be said that many of the shepherds who wandered into that trackless wilderness never returned to biblical Christianity, and they sadly drew many ordinary people in after them.

On the other hand, the collapse of mainline Protestantism has also produced good side effects. There is today much less "cultural Christianity" in English Canada, in the sense that there are fewer people who think they are a Christian because they vaguely remember that their grandmother was an Anglican. Today, the veneer of inherited Anglican, United, or Presbyterian identity has mostly been peeled away, with the result that such people now think of themselves as simply having "no religion." The new situation is much clearer, and provides opportunities for people to hear the gospel afresh.

The decline of mainline Protestantism has also curtailed the influence of liberal Protestant theology, which is not often found outside the dwindling mainline churches and seminaries (except perhaps in certain corners of the universities). The result is a much sharper and clearer line between belief and unbelief,

---

justice and uprightness of Titus and Trajan were no better than the rage and cruelty of Caligula, Nero, and Domitian." John Calvin, *The Institutes of Christian Religion*, edited by Tony Lane and Hilary Osborne (Grand Rapids, MI: Baker Academic, 1987), 3.14.2.

between orthodox Christianity and modern atheism. All of this is a silver lining for those who want to proclaim the gospel clearly to their neighbours today.

So much for the mixed results of the changes in mainline Protestantism. What about the changes in evangelicalism? First, and most positively, the growth of evangelical churches and ministries outside the mainline meant that there continued to be a strong, orthodox Protestant voice for Jesus, the Bible, and the gospel in Canada despite the breakdown of the mainline churches. Although this growth was by no means enough to offset numerically the losses of churchgoers from the mainline, God did not leave himself without a faithful witness in this country. And when men and women of evangelical convictions decided to leave the mainline churches, there was a place for them to go where they could hear preaching based on the authority of God's word and be equipped for lives of holiness, witness, and service. The faithfulness of these churches to the gospel meant that the centre of gravity of Protestantism in Canada at the end of the century was once again an *evangelical* one after a hundred years or more of liberal ascendancy.

The willingness of evangelicals to cooperate in speaking publicly also meant that there was a voice for biblical values in the public square. At the end of the century, evangelicals vied with conservative Catholics for the honour of being the strongest voice for the sanctity of life, freedom of religion and conscience, the educational rights of parents, and the importance of marriage for society. Although the overall trends on each of these issues at the end of the century were not what evangelicals would have hoped, evangelical engagement with them did lead to significant accomplishments—both symbolic results, like the inclusion of a reference to God in the preamble to the *Charter of Rights and Freedoms*, and practical results, like the Supreme Court's ruling in favour of Trinity Western University when the British Columbia College of Teachers tried to shut out its graduates.

However, as alluded to earlier, this public role was also fraught with temptations. Entering into coalitions and conversations in the halls of power, the need to appear credible, the desire to come across as good citizens and team players—all of these things, understandable and even necessary in themselves, made it easier for evangelical leaders to slip into a preoccupation with "how they see us," and following from that, an unhealthy tendency to downplay those elements of evangelical teaching and heritage that were not acceptable in polite circles. At worst, it could lead to a craving for the world's approval and acceptance. Now, such temptations were not equally strong everywhere. They were perhaps felt most keenly by professors in Christian universities whose graduate school training had socialized them into the rituals and the standards and even the values of the secular academy. Again, we should not be quick to judge, nor do we need to throw the baby out with the bathwater. Nevertheless, at the end of the twentieth century, the pressures, especially on issues of sexuality and gender, were only increasing, and there were unsettling parallels between current-day trends in evangelicalism and the initial rise of liberalism in the mainline churches 130 years earlier. Moreover, there were signs that the vigour of evangelical churches, at least as measured in terms of growth, was levelling off in the early part of the twenty-first century.[63] Would evangelicals accept their status as strangers and exiles on

---

[63] Sam Reimer, "Evangelical Denominational and Congregational Growth in Canada," paper presented at the annual meeting of the Society for the Scientific Study of Religion and the Religious Research Association, Boston, Massachusetts, November 7–10, 2013.

the earth, or would they follow the well-trodden path of respectability, liberalism, and fatal compromise?[64]

Put differently, what would our hypothetical time-traveller find if he or she returned another century hence? Despite the uncertainties of the future, for evangelicals—always a Bible people—there was comfort to be found in knowing that, whatever winds would blow, and whatever seas may rise, they believed in a God who could calm the storms and part the waters.

---

[64] John Stackhouse was already asking these sorts of questions at the beginning of the 1990s; see *Canadian Evangelicalism*, 203-204.

3

CHURCH AND STATE: GOSPEL IMPERATIVES

Kirk Wellum

In the previous essays, we have read about Canada's spiritual past and how we have arrived in our present situation. Now it is time to ask the question: *Where do we go from here?*

All of the participants in the conference, and all of the contributors to this book, believe that whatever we say by way of counsel and exhortation must be rooted in the Bible. To that end, I want to address the question of where we go from here by looking at the seven letters to the seven churches that are recorded in Revelation 2-3.[1]

By way of introduction, we should observe that the seven churches were real historical churches that existed in first-century Asia Minor. But more than that, because the letters are addressed to seven churches in a prophetic book that is full of

---

[1] I want to acknowledge my indebtedness to: G. K. Beale, *The Book of Revelation* (Grand Rapids, MI: W. B. Eerdmans Publishing Co., 1999); William Hendriksen, *More Than Conquerors* (Grand Rapids: Baker Books, 1998); Jonathan Menn, *Biblical Eschatology*, Second ed., (Searcy, AR: Resource Publications, 2018); Robert H. Mounce, *The Book of Revelation*, NICNT (Grand Rapids, MI: W. B. Eerdmans Publishing Co., 1977); Grant R. Osborne, *Revelation*, BECNT (Grand Rapids: Baker Academic, 2002); Anthony A. Hoekema, *The Bible and the Future* (Grand Rapids, MI: W. B. Eerdmans, 1994); and the Study Notes in the NIV and ESV Study Bibles ad loc.

symbolism, the churches should also be viewed as representative of Christian congregations that exist on earth during the gospel age, until Jesus Christ comes again.[2] Practically, this means that in Revelation 2–3 we have messages to seven historical churches through whom the Spirit speaks to the worldwide church throughout history, even down to present day Canada in which we live.[3]

Looking at the seven letters as a group, Beale observes that they can be divided into 3 groups—those who are in danger of extinction unless they repent, those who are faithful to the Lord in spite of the hardships they are facing, and those whose character is a combination of good things and evil things, the latter needing to be dealt with immediately.[4] Further confirmation of the 3 groups is found by Beale in a chiastic "a-b-c-c-b-a" structure that orders the way the letters are presented based on the spiritual condition of the churches. Thus, the first church in Ephesus and the last church in Laodicea are threatened with extinction if they do not repent; the churches in Smyrna and Philadelphia are faithful even though they are suffering persecution; and the churches in Pergamum, Thyatira, and Sardis are a mix of good things and things that must change to avoid the Lord's discipline and judgment.[5]

---

[2] By *gospel age* I am referring to what is sometimes called the interadvental period, or the time between the first and second advents of Christ. Whatever one chooses to call it, it is the time in which we now live in redemptive history.

[3] Note the repetition of "what the Spirit says to the churches" at the end of each letter (Revelation 2:7, 11, 17, 29; 3:8, 13, 22), and the plural usage of the word "churches" which may indicate that the Spirit is speaking to all Christian assemblies. Cf. Mounce, *Revelation*, 83–84.

[4] Beale, *Revelation*, 226.

[5] Beale, *Revelation*, 226–227.

Taken together the letters help us see the challenges we must wrestle with as Christians until Jesus returns at the end of the age. This is true wherever the church is found, including Canada. In one sense there is nothing new under the sun, but in another, old challenges reappear dressed in new clothes and utilizing a modified vocabulary. By studying the letters, we learn what to expect and how the Lord wants us to respond to the challenges embedded in this epoch in redemptive history.

If we are to correctly interpret and apply the letters to our current situation we must, 1) understand the historical situation in first-century Asia Minor, 2) understand how the letters draw upon previous biblical revelation, especially the Old Testament scriptures, and how they interpret the Old Testament in light of the coming of Jesus and the establishment of his kingdom, and 3) understand the challenges of the present age towards the gospel. We must also be conscious of the positioning of the letters within the book of Revelation and the influence they exert on the rest of the book. Notably, they come after the *Son of Man* vision in 1:9-20, which provides biblical and eschatological context for the letters, and, taken together, chapters 1-3 set the stage for what follows in chapters 4-22.[6]

The consistency in the flow and structure of the letters is also noteworthy. In each letter, Jesus presents himself to the church in a way that is appropriate to their unique situation, the churches are reviewed positively and negatively, divine kingly counsel is promulgated, a call to respond is issued, and finally a promise of eternal life is given in a way relevant to each church.[7]

At the risk of being reductionistic, I will seek to capture the essence of each ecclesial situation to learn how we should parse our present predicament and how we should proceed. We should

---

[6] Beale, *Revelation*, 224, 311-312.
[7] Beale, *Revelation*, 224-225; Mounce, *Revelation*, 84.

note that only two of the seven churches are "faithful," while all the rest have significant, life-threatening problems that must be dealt with if they are to survive and be what God calls them to be in the world. We also must note that there is no "one size fits all" solution and each congregation receives personal attention from the Lord. As we proceed, we will see that there is a fascinating connection between the spiritual condition of the churches and the religious, social, and sometimes even geographical characteristics of the cities in which they were located, reminding us that we must never underestimate the influence of our surroundings.

The Church in Ephesus (2:1–7): Orthodox but Loveless

The first church addressed is located in the city of Ephesus, which, in the first century, was the fourth largest city in the Roman Empire and had political, commercial, and geographical importance.[8] It was known in the ancient world for its massive temple to the goddess Artemis, as well as for the worship of Demetrius, the practice of sorcery, idolatry, and the worship of the Roman Emperor.[9] We know from Acts 19 that the apostle Paul did evangelistic and apologetic work there for two years, using the lecture hall of Tyrannus as a base for his ministry. Paul's protégé, Timothy, also ministered there, as did the apostle John. Ephesus also seems to have been strategic in terms of Paul's ministry to the Gentiles in Asia Minor.

In his letter, Jesus identifies himself to the church as the one who "holds the seven stars or angels in his right hand and walks

---

[8] Mounce, *Revelation*, 85–86; Osborne, *Revelation*, 108–110; *NIV Zondervan Study Bible*, 2590.

[9] See Acts 19; Beale, *Revelation*, 223–224; Mounce, *Revelation*, 86; *NIV Study Bible* and *ESV Study Bible* ad loc.

among the seven golden lampstands" (2:1). In 1:20 he explains that the seven golden lampstands represent the churches (1:20).[10] This means that Jesus is among his people as the resurrected God-man and, as such, he knows them and he can help them in their time of need. He begins by enumerating what is praiseworthy about them as a congregation. For instance, he knows their deeds, hard work, and perseverance and he knows that they have not grown weary. They are passionate about truth and intolerant of those who espouse false doctrine and false practices. The believers in Ephesus have tested those who claim to be apostles but are not, and they have found them false. Later he commends them for hating the practices of the Nicolaitans, which he also hates.

This positive assessment is supported and illustrated by what is said in Acts 20:28-30 regarding the church in Ephesus. In that passage Paul warns the church about teachers who will come after his departure and will try to draw away disciples after themselves. Consequently, they must be on their guard and hold fast to the whole will of God that Paul proclaimed to them. Later, when he writes to Timothy, who had a position of leadership in the Ephesian church, he emphasizes the importance of truth in connection with elders, deacons, and the congregation, because the church is "the pillar and foundation of the truth" (1 Tim. 1:15). Still later in the same correspondence he warns about people abandoning the faith and following things taught by demons (4:1-8), and urges Timothy to teach and insist on what is consistent with sound, Christ-centered instruction and godly

---

[10] "Angels" probably does not represent the ministers of the churches but angelic representatives of the congregations. See Beale, *Revelation*, 217-219. Cf. Mounce, *Revelation*, 85, "The reference is to the prevailing spirit of the church rather than to the guardian angel or ruling official of the congregation."

teaching (6:2-3). In 2 Timothy there are similar warnings about what will happen in "the last days," followed by a powerful exhortation to "preach the word; be prepared in season and out of season; correct, rebuke and encourage—with great patience and careful instruction" (2 Tim. 3:1-9; 3:10-4:5). From what is said in Revelation 2:1-7 it is apparent that the church in Ephesus took Paul's teaching to heart.

But despite their passionate concern and defense of the truth, Jesus tells them that "they have forsaken the love they had at first" (2:4). The precise meaning of this charge is debated. Some argue that Jesus is talking about their *love for God*, and undoubtedly there is an element of truth in that. Others think he is talking about their *love for one another*, and still others their *love for the world*. Again, I think there is something to be said for all of these suggestions and it is difficult to isolate them from one another. Beale suggests something more specific considering the *lampstand* imagery that is employed by Jesus in his introduction (2:1), and the judgment that is threatened near the end of the letter in the event of noncompliance (2:5). He suggests that they have lost the love they had at first in that they are not witnessing to the surrounding world as they should. In this they have become like Israel under the Old Covenant who failed to be a light to the nations.[11]

Regardless of the precise meaning, if they do not "consider how far they have fallen and repent and do the things that they did at first, the Lord will come and remove their lampstand from its place" (2:5). This reminds us that love for God which reveals itself in many ways, including Christian witness, is crucial for the

---

[11] Beale, *Revelation*, 230-231. Cf. Mounce, *Revelation*, 89, "Without love the congregation ceases to be a church. Its lampstand is removed."

church and not an optional extra. If a church merely exists to meet its own needs, the Lord himself will shut it down. Proclaiming the gospel and living it out before others is something that only Christians can do, and it is urgently needed in our country today. Faithfulness in this regard is not easy in the current climate of "political-correctness" and "moral signaling," and it may prove to be downright dangerous in terms of career advancement or getting access to government money that we may be entitled to as tax-paying citizens. But the command and expectation of our Lord is clear—we must be lights shining in the darkness. Truth and love must go together. Right doctrine and practice must never be severed. Ours is a day of profound biblical illiteracy and now, more than ever, we need to shine in a warped and crooked generation like stars in the sky, as we hold firmly to the word of life (Phil. 2:15-16).

The Church in Smyrna (2:8-11):
Afflicted, Poor, Slandered, yet Faithful

The second church addressed was located in the ancient city of Smyrna, which is modern-day Izmir, and is located 56 km north of Ephesus. In the first century it was a beautiful city with paved streets, a library, and a gymnasium. In previous years the city had died only to be revived and restored in more recent times (600-290 BC). As the birthplace of Homer, with a shrine dedicated to his honor, it was a city with an abundant amount of civic pride. Both the Roman Emperor and the goddess Roma were worshipped in Smyrna.[12] It should be noted that the city also had a significant Jewish population. But according to our Lord, it was a city in which his people experienced a significant degree of

---

[12] See *NIV Study Bible*, 2591; *ESV Study Bible*, 2466. Cf. Mounce, *Revelation*, 73-74; Beale, *Revelation*, 240-241; Osborne, *Revelation*, 127-128.

persecution, and the reason for this persecution is probably tied to the way in which the gospel spread in the first century world.

Initially, when the Christian gospel broke into the world, Christian communities were viewed as subsets of Judaism and therefore enjoyed exemptions afforded to the Jews by the governing authorities because of their religious beliefs and concerns over idolatrous defilement. But as Christians were pushed out of the synagogues because of their teachings about Jesus, they no longer enjoyed the protection of the "Jewish umbrella" and this expulsion brought them into direct conflict with the Roman authorities. Such conflict was problematic because access to public monies were tied to the worship of the emperor, and this was something that Christians could not do. Non-participation was considered unpatriotic and disloyalty made persecution justifiable from a Roman point of view. Such persecution is what inevitably happened to those who had sworn exclusive allegiance to Jesus.[13]

In his letter to the church in Smyrna, Jesus introduces himself as "the First and the Last, who died and came to life again" (2:8). This description is intended to remind them of important truths that they must not forget in such a hostile environment. The "First and the Last" speaks of his eternal nature—he was there in the beginning and he will be there in the end. Furthermore, it tells us that he is sovereign over history—all of it is known to him and under his control. And what is more, he died, but has come to life again! And as someone who has triumphed over death, he is able to help his persecuted people. Elsewhere Paul indicates that Jesus' resurrection from the dead puts him in a class by himself and indicates that the times have turned and

---

[13] Beale, *Revelation*, 240-241.

GOSPEL IMPERATIVES

all power belongs to him as the resurrected God-man (cf. Phil. 2:6-11; Col. 1:15-20).

It is not surprising, then, that he knows all about their situation: "He knows their afflictions and poverty—yet they are rich!" They possess true riches even though the world might not see it that way. He also "knows the slander of those who say they are Jews and are not but are a synagogue of Satan." Behind this provocative assessment and critique is the redemptive-historical fact that the *people of God* have been redefined by the true Israel, the Lord Jesus Christ.[14] Like their Lord, these believers are called to suffer. Some will face prison, and most likely death, since incarceration for its own sake was rare in the first century. However, their sufferings will not go on indefinitely, but rather will have a limited duration described in terms of "ten days;" that may harken back to Daniel 1, and the testing of the Hebrew exiles Daniel, Hananiah, Mishael and Azariah in Babylon (Dan. 1:6, 12-13).[15] Their experience of significant but temporary suffering is typical of the gospel age in which we live. In this environment faithfulness is required: A faithfulness engendered by keeping our eyes on Jesus, the resurrected one, who will give his faithful one the crown which is life—or immunity from the second death.

Like our brothers and sisters in Smyrna, we may be called on to suffer for the Lord. Living in Canada, many of us have never experienced the kind of persecution that other Christians face in countries where they live. This is a great mercy and we

---

[14] Cf. Genesis 3:15; Matthew 2:15; John 8:39-44 and many other passages talk about two divisions of humanity from the very beginning—those who are the seed of the woman versus the seed of the serpent. Jesus is the true and ultimate Son of God and Israel, and only those who are related to him by faith are true Israelites. Cf., Romans 2:28-29; 9:6-24; Galatians 4:21-31; 6:16.

[15] Beale, *Revelation*, 242.

should be thankful for it. But freedom from persecution is not promised to us in this life. Persecution is often the norm rather than the exception. As we celebrate the 150th anniversary of Canada, there are growing storm clouds on the horizon when it comes to the toleration of biblical truth in our society. Many of us feel that we are witnessing a significant apostasy and a turning away from historic Christianity and the freedoms it has generated. If this declension continues unchecked, we will face persecution in a way most of us have never faced before. If and when that happens, we must remember that it will not last forever, nor will it destroy the cause of Christ. Jesus has triumphed, and so will we! His victory over the forces allied against him means that we must face these temporary troubles with resiliency, calmness, and determination.

The Church in Pergamum (2:12-17):
External Vigilance, Internal Compromise

The third church addressed by Jesus was in the ancient city of Pergamum. It had a population of approximately 100,000 people and was situated 113 km north of Smyrna. Pergamum was an amazing inland city that had a 200,000-volume library, a religious centre with a 40-foot-high statue of Zeus, a shrine to Asclepios, the serpent god of healing, as well as shrines to Athena, Demeter, and Dionysus. It was also the centre of the Roman government in that area with its accompanying emperor cult and the idolatry that went along with it. Indicative of its political significance, Pergamum was the warden of Caesar's temple and the first city to build a temple to a Roman ruler, in this case,

Augustus.[16] These characteristics of the city help explain why Jesus describes it as the place "where Satan lives."[17]

When Jesus writes to the church, he introduces himself as the one "who has the sharp, doubled-edged sword." The reference to the sword may signify that he has authority to rule and execute judgment. This also means that here, as elsewhere, he comes as one who *knows*—he knows where they live, and he knows what they are dealing with in their lives. But more than that, he also knows that they remain true to his name despite the spiritually hostile environment in which they reside. As an example, he speaks of their faith in him, even in the days of Antipas, who he describes as "my faithful witness," who was put to death in the city—where Satan lives. The repetition of that last phrase probably indicates that there were intense spiritual challenges and manifestations of evil in the city that made it difficult to live as a Christian.

But for all their faithfulness during various trials, there was a problem in the church. There were some who held to the teaching of Balaam and the Nicolaitans. Balaam was a false prophet who, motivated by greed, was hired by the Moabite enemies of Israel to curse Israel as a people (cf. Numbers 22:1-25:3; 31:8, 16). When he was unable to do so because of the Lord's intervention, he told Balak, the Moabite king, how to lead Israel astray by enticing them to engage in immorality and idolatry. The precise nature of the teachings of the Nicolaitans is not known, but some scholars say their name means "the victory people."[18]

---

[16] *NIV Study Bible*, 2591. Cf. Mounce, *Revelation*, 77-79; Osborne, *Revelation*, 138-139.

[17] Beale, *Revelation*, 246-247.

[18] *NIV Study Bible*, note on 2:6; cf. Beale, *Revelation*, 251. Also see Mounce, *Revelation*, 98, "If the first four words are to be taken as a unit, it follows that the Nicolaitans are essentially the same group as the Balaamites. Both describe an antinomian group which had

This designation might indicate that they were espousing some type of heretical teaching or practice that promised spiritual victory in the lives of those who adhered to their false teaching. But whatever the precise nature of their teaching, Jesus is concerned about internal spiritual compromise. For example, these false teachers may have suggested something along the lines of "let's be practical about this," and then advocated for some sort of pragmatic compromise as a way of dealing with persecution. Regardless of whatever the specific teachings were, it resulted in the corruption of the gospel and holy living, and had to be dealt with before any more harm was done.

Those who have gone astray are called to repent and are warned that if they do not, the Lord himself will come and fight against them with the sword of his mouth. The *sword* reference is interesting in this context because, in the Old Testament story of Balaam, Balaam was confronted by the angel of the Lord with a drawn sword as he was on his way to meet Israel's enemies.[19] The Lord spared Balaam's life on that occasion, but he will not spare those who are leading the church astray. The Lord is jealous for the purity of his people and we should be too. In the church today, we cannot remain faithful to him while simultaneously tolerating ideas or practices that are clearly contrary to what is expected of us as his people as revealed in his word. In the Canadian context we are often reluctant to deal with departures from biblical teaching in the name of love and unity. While these graces are important, error will harm the church if allowed to spread unchecked. We must return to the Scriptures when the secular culture tempts us to look the other way or to be more open-minded. Today, the confusion surrounding the nature of

---

accommodated itself to the religious and social requirements of the pagan society in which they lived."

[19] Numbers 22:23, 31.

marriage, what it means to be a man or a woman, and similar issues must not be overlooked or downplayed. The culture seems to have gone mad and is trying to reverse long established standards of right and wrong. We must not allow this madness to contaminate the bride of Christ.

To encourage the believers in Pergamum to keep the course, and those who have gone astray to repent, Jesus promises to give those who are victorious *hidden manna*; that is, food that sustains and food that speaks of fellowship with God enjoyed in this life, after death, and ultimately in the consummation at the end of the age.[20] To these same people he will also give a "white stone with a new name written on it known only to the one who receives it." In the ancient world, a white stone was sometimes used to indicate acquittal in a legal case or used as a token to secure admission into an event.[21]

Whatever the exact meaning here, both acquittal and admission represent a symbolic reversal of the decision of the world, so that the person who is judged guilty or inadmissible by the world is instead welcomed into the presence of God. No matter what anyone says today, those who are on the Lord's side are on the right side of history, and those who capitulate to the current apostasy will find themselves on the outside looking in unless they quickly change their course.

---

[20] Cf. Mounce, *Revelation*, 99, "In the context of the letter to Pergamum it alludes to the proper and heavenly food of spiritual Israel in contrast to the unclean food supplied by the Balaamites. While the promise is primarily eschatological, it is not without immediate application for a persecuted people."

[21] Beale, *Revelation*, 253.

The Church in Thyatira (2:18-29):
Love, Faith, Service, Perseverance, but Devilish Error

The fourth church addressed by Jesus was in the city of Thyatira, which was 64 km southeast of Pergamum. It was the home of many trade guilds, each with its own deity, which often spelled trouble for Christians who confessed Jesus as their Lord. According to Acts 16:14, Thyatira was also the home of a woman named Lydia, who was a dealer in purple cloth. Luke, the author of Acts, tells us that she was converted to Christ because of the evangelistic ministry of the apostle Paul in that city. Of all the cities addressed in Revelation 2-3, Thyatira was the least important, yet it receives the longest message.[22] Things are not always as they appear when looked at in light of the kingdom of God.

To the church in Thyatira, Jesus introduces himself as "the Son of God whose eyes are like blazing fire and whose feet are like burnished bronze." The phrase "Son of God" is not found in the vision of the "son of man" in 1:13-15, although given the close connection between the opening vision and the diverse ways Jesus introduces himself to the churches, some suggest it may be an expository explanation of the phrase "son of man" in chapter 1.[23] If this is the intent, it implies that the "son of man" is also the "Son of God." This is fascinating because the latter reference takes us back to Daniel 3 and the mysterious visitant (a son of the gods) who walked with Shadrack, Meshach, and Abednego in Nebuchadnezzar's fiery furnace, as well as to Psalm 2 and the messianic Son who is installed as king of Zion, God's holy mountain. Jesus is all of this, and more. He is the one with

---

[22] *NIV Study Bible*, 2592. Cf. Mounce, *Revelation*, 101-102; Osborne, *Revelation*, 151-152.

[23] Beale, *Revelation*, 259.

authority, and consequently his word and judgment are final, and the church should always keep this in mind.[24]

As such, he "knows their deeds—their love, faith, service, and perseverance." He knows that "they are now doing more than they did at first." In this, they were doing better than the church in Ephesus who declined in their pursuit of God, activity, and zeal as time went on. But, for all these good things, there was a notable problem. In the church was a false prophetess and her followers, identified here as "Jezebel and her children."[25] She was operating in the church and had been for some time. In Revelation, false prophecy is connected to the beast that comes out of the earth; a beast that has two horns like a lamb, but it speaks like a dragon.[26] In other words, false prophecy and those who speak it are beastly.

Consistent with its character, false prophecy is dangerous, deceptive, and leads people astray into immorality and idolatry. Perhaps we can gain some insight into the way false prophecy was being presented by looking at what Jesus says about those who have "not learned Satan's so-called deep secrets." This suggests that the false teachers were claiming clever, insider-exclusive knowledge. They were taking anyone who would listen beyond what had been revealed by God's apostles and prophets, and supposedly letting them in on deep secrets that God had not disclosed. But for all their arrogant promises, the result was the same as in Pergamum. They were leading people astray and they are told that if they did not repent, they would be severely punished. The Lord's truth will prevail in his church.

Today we have teachers who think they are too sophisticated for the Bible. They openly question what the Bible teaches

---

[24] Beale, *Revelation*, 259.
[25] 1 Kings 16; 21; 2 Kings 9.
[26] Revelation 13:11–17.

and what historic Christianity has always affirmed about such things as the historicity of Adam, the inspiration of the Old and New Testaments, the vicarious substitutionary nature of Christ's atonement, the eternal punishment of the wicked, and the absolute sovereignty of God over all things. Some influential pastors, teachers, and writers act as if these remnants from a bygone era must be updated in view of current scholarship and cynicism. This departure from the truth is especially subtle when it is wrapped in apparent concern for apologetic relevance. The unwarranted reinterpretation of Scripture, however, no matter how superficially clever, is theologically equivalent to the false prophecy in Thyatira and must be refuted and rejected.

Given the situation with Jezebel and her followers, Jesus tells the church in Thyatira "to hold on to what they have until he comes" (2:25). This means that they are not to innovate but are rather to teach and believe the apostolic gospel that had been delivered to them! This is the only way to escape the judgment which will fall on Jezebel and her brood. From the time the serpent beguiled Eve in Eden, error is often peddled as deep, innovative, or sophisticated thought, but when examined in the light of Scripture we come to see that this is not the case.

As an encouragement to hold on to what they have, those who are victorious and do the will of Jesus to the end are promised authority to rule with him. In fulfillment of Psalm 2—alluded to earlier—Jesus has already begun to reign and we share in that reign now and, in even greater measure, in the age to come.[27] The authority of Jesus is underscored by reference to *the morning star*, which is picked up and repeated at the end of

---

[27] Cf. Beale, *Revelation*, 266-267, "Concluding with the promise of Psalm 2 is fitting since Christ introduced himself at the beginning of the letter as 'the Son of God,' a title derived from Psalm 2, which affirms further that he has begun to fulfill the prophecy of the Psalm."

the prophecy in Revelation 22:16.[28] The long-awaited king has come and has begun to reign, and we reign with him now, and in the future, as we remain true to his Word that has been once for all revealed in the scriptures.

The Church in Sardis (3:1-6):
Living in the Past and out of Touch with Reality

The fifth church addressed was in Sardis, 56 kilometers southeast of Thyatira. In the first century, it was also home to a large and influential Jewish population. From an economic standpoint, both Sardis and Philadelphia had been severely damaged by an earthquake in 17 AD and had been rebuilt with help from the Romans. Sardis had a theater, a stadium, and a central road made of marble, along with many temples. There was an unfinished temple to Artemis in the city that provides some structural context for what Jesus will say to the church.

Historically and geographically, it is also important to know that the city had a glorious past and a reputation for being impregnable due to its elevated and rocky location. But despite this natural advantage, the city's defenses had been breached twice, once by Cyrus II in 546 BC and again by Antiochus III in 214 BC. On both occasions the watchmen were caught off-guard and, as a result, the city was captured.[29]

When Jesus speaks to them he does so as "the one who holds the seven spirits of God and the seven stars!" In other words, he is telling them that he is the head of the church, full of the Spirit, the captain of the heavenly host, and he can help. He knows their deeds and reputation for being alive, but, in fact,

---

[28] Cf. Numbers 24:15-19 and Isaiah 11:1. Cf. Beale, *Revelation*, 268-269.

[29] Mounce, *Revelation*, 108-109; Osborne, *Revelation*, 171-172. Cf. *NIV Study Bible*, 2593.

they are dead. Here is a group of people who are living in the past, remembering the glory days gone by as if they were still living in them. What is urgently needed, therefore, is for them to "wake up!" They need to "strengthen what remains and is about to die." In addition, they must "remember what they have received and hold it fast and repent."

If they fail to do as Jesus prescribes, they will be disciplined when Jesus comes in judgment. This judgment will catch them unaware, just as the city in days gone by was caught unaware, because he will come like a thief, or at a time when they least expect it. This judgment in history is part of the last great judgment that will happen at the end of history, but it is already present in a preliminary form. It is as though judgment begins with the church and the people of God, and then extends out into the world.

Even though some are living in the past, there is a remnant in the church who have not soiled their clothes. This is one reason why judgment is necessary. The church must be purified and cleansed because this is consistent with the nature of the church as a New Covenant community. As a New Covenant community it is not a spiritually mixed multitude of believers and unbelievers, but rather a group of people who have been redeemed by the Lamb and renewed by the Holy Spirit. Those who are faithful will walk with the Lord and be dressed in white and their names will never be blotted from the book of life (cf. 20:11-12). They will be acknowledged before the Father and his angels—the highest form of recognition.

In Canada today, we must be prepared to do what is right in the eyes of the Lord even if it is out of step with what the culture thinks is good, right, and desirable. We cannot let the worldview of secular people define how we think and function as Christians. Christian leaders need to make sure they are grounded in the truth of God's Word and they need to challenge their congregations to hold on to the same truth and let it shape their lives. Even if we never receive acclaim in this life, this letter assures us that we will be recognized by the Lord in the age to come.

The Church in Philadelphia (3:7-13):
Small but Mighty

Philadelphia was located 48 km southeast of Sardis and today it is modern Ataşehir in Turkey. It was an important commercial city that was strategically located on commercial trade routes. It also had temples that were dedicated to Zeus and to the Roman Emperor and it shared in the paganism of the day. Like Sardis it was rebuilt by the Romans after it had been devastated by the earthquake in 17 AD, and it was re-named Neo-Caesarea in recognition of the financial assistance supplied by Rome.[30] In this religious and political context, the church faced pressure from the pagan culture as well as what Jesus calls "the synagogue of Satan"—a group who claimed to be Jews but, in a full New Covenant and eschatological sense, were not.

Jesus addresses the church in Philadelphia as one "who is holy and true, who holds the key of David, so that what he opens no one can shut, and what he shuts no one can open." This is a cryptic reference to Isaiah 22:2-22, and when Jesus employs it, he is teaching us that he fulfills the role of Eliakim, while the believers in Philadelphia are like those who inhabited Jerusalem and Judah in Isaiah's day. In other words, Jesus, who is the ultimate fulfillment of Isaiah's prophecy, has the power to save and the power to judge.[31] He is the one who is in control and the believers in Philadelphia must remember that, even though they

---

[30] Mounce, *Revelation*, 114-115; Osborne, *Revelation*, 184-186. Cf. *NIV Study Bible*, 2594.

[31] Beale, *Revelation*, 283-285.

are viewed as insignificant by the world. Like the church in Smyrna, he has no word of criticism for them. Instead, he encourages them to remain faithful and to fulfill their calling.

As the head of the church, Jesus tells them that he knows their deeds and has placed before them an open door that no one can shut. He will bless their labors and they will be successful. Though they are small and have little strength—little of this world's resources—they have kept his Word and have not denied his name. They have been faithful in difficult circumstances and he will look after them. He will bring those who are of the synagogue of Satan, those who claim to be Jews but are liars, to fall down at the believers' feet as Jesus acknowledges his love for his people in Philadelphia—and beyond! Those who imagine that they are *true Israel* will see that they are mistaken, unless they surrender to Jesus. They, and we, must realize that he acknowledges as his loved ones those who obey his Word even though they are despised by the world.

The Lord also promises to keep them from the hour of trial that will come on the whole world to test the inhabitants of the earth. This does not necessarily mean they will be exempt from trial, but more likely that they will experience trouble as well as blessing, and in the end, they will be safe. Given these divine promises, they must hold on to what they have so that no one will take their crown. If they hold fast, they are promised a place in the temple of God—not the earthly temple in Jerusalem that has already been destroyed, but the ultimate temple of God; that is, the new Jerusalem where God will dwell with his people forever, and where they will bear his new name.

According to The Evangelical Fellowship of Canada, only 8–12% of Canadians are Evangelicals.[32] Even if we may

---

[32] See https://www.evangelicalfellowship.ca/About-us/About-Evangelicals (accessed May 12, 2018).

legitimately argue over the accuracy of these numbers, when it comes to those who are orthodox, confessional Christians, the research shows that we represent a small percentage of the Canadian population. As such we may be tempted to wonder what we can realistically do to make a difference. Jesus' words to the believers in Philadelphia teach us that it is not by human might or power but rather it is by God's might and power that evil strongholds are defeated and the church advances.[33] We must not be discouraged, but instead faithfully fulfill God's calling for our lives by testifying to his goodness and grace, and leave the results to him.

The Church in Laodicea (3:14-21):
Rich, Smug, and Nauseating

The last church addressed was in the city of Laodicea, 72 km southeast of Philadelphia. It was destroyed by an earthquake in 60 AD but it was rebuilt with private money and not public funds, as in the cases of Sardis and Philadelphia. The private rebuild was possible because the city was prosperous with thriving financial, medical, and textile industries. Laodicea also boasted two theaters and a stadium, and like many of the other cities, it was a place where Zeus was worshiped, as well as another deity known as Men Karou, the god of healing and patron of the medical school. But for all of its wealth, Laodicea had serious water problems. The Lycus River near the city was muddy, rendering the water undrinkable, and therefore water had to be brought into the city from somewhere else. To remedy the situation, an aqueduct was built that carried water 8 km from hot springs in the south. Not only was the water lukewarm by the time it arrived in Laodicea, but the water did not taste very good after

---

[33] See Matthew 16:13-20, cf. Zechariah 4:6.

coming that distance in the aqueduct. This local water problem plays prominently into what Jesus says to the church in the city.[34]

Jesus presents himself to the church in Laodicea as "the Amen, the faithful and true witness, and the ruler of God's creation." In doing so he is reminding them that he is the "Yes" of God, the foundation and standard of all revelation, the ruler and beginning (in the sense of preeminent agent) of God's creation. As such he knows their deeds and is qualified to render judgment.

What follows is an extended critique without any words of praise. Laodicea is unenviably unique in this regard, a fact that was probably embarrassing to this proud church. Jesus begins by telling them that he knows that they are neither hot nor cold and, in his assessment, it would be better if they were one or the other because, as they stand, their lukewarmness warrants spitting them out of his mouth. Contrary to some interpreters and some popular preaching, Jesus is not putting a premium on being cold or indifferent when it comes to his reign. Rather, he is using the water problem that existed in the city to charge that they were neither of medicinal value (hot), nor were they refreshing (cold), but instead they were nauseatingly lukewarm, and therefore good for nothing but to be spit out![35]

Ironically, the church in Laodicea did not share Jesus' evaluation of their spiritual condition. They saw themselves as wealthy and as not needing anything. But Jesus, knowing their true spiritual state, says that they do not realize that they are wretched, pitiful, poor, blind, and naked. This likely indicates

---

[34] Mounce, *Revelation*, 122-124; Osborne, *Revelation*, 201-203. Cf. *NIV Study Bible*, 2595.

[35] See Beale, *Revelation*, 303; Mounce, *Revelation*, 125; Osborne, *Revelation*, 206.

that they have been unfaithful to their calling and have thoroughly compromised, even though they do not see it that way.

Jesus continues on to say that if the church in Laodicea is to avoid judgment and dissolution, they must buy gold refined in the fire, so that they can become rich. This is an appropriately graphic way of saying that they need to seek true riches that will not contaminate them but will rather stand the test when they pass through the judgment. They are to buy white clothes to wear so they can cover their shameful nakedness. Their own clothes, as fine as they are, are inadequate and leave them exposed in the presence of the Lord. The recipients of the Lord's rebuke need to put on purity and holiness, which are the best adornments. They are also to put salve on their eyes so that they can see. Their vision is distorted, their values inverted, and their pride is in their shame. They need to re-evaluate their entire position before it is too late.[36]

Lest they think Jesus is being too harsh with them, he reminds them that he rebukes and disciplines those he loves. It is never a good thing when we are allowed to get away with sin and rebellion. On the contrary, it is an expression of God's grace and mercy when he confronts us and calls us to be earnest and repent. Here in this letter the Lord comes to his people and pleads with them to hear his voice and open the door. If they do, he will come in and eat with them and they with him. It is a wonderful picture of fellowship restored.

And as if this were not enough, to the one who is victorious Jesus gives the right to sit with him on his throne, just as he was victorious and sat down with his Father on his throne. Once

---

[36] The prescription of Jesus is framed in terms that the residents of Laodicea would immediately understand because the city was well known for its wealth, glossy black wool, and a medical centre that had developed its own eye salve. See Osborne, *Revelation*, 206–210.

again there is the promise of sharing in his rule even now in this world, and more so in the world to come.

As Christians living in a very affluent country at this point in history, the letter to the Laodicean church is particularly challenging. It is so easy to misread our own spiritual condition and think that we are better off than we are because of the many privileges we enjoy in Canada. We need to remember that the greatest blessing belongs to those who know the Lord and who glory in him as their Lord and Savior.

In this chapter we have seen that the seven letters to the seven churches are written to Christian churches wherever they are scattered throughout the world during the gospel age. These missives speak to the particular struggles that we have in the world as Christians seeking to live under the authority of Jesus. Until he comes we must remember the priority of love, faithfulness in persecution, doctrinal and moral purity, the need to hold fast to what we have, and to stay awake and moving forward, never forgetting that if we have the Lord on our side we have all that we need. We must also remember the importance of humility and authenticity as we serve and worship our exalted Lord. It is my prayer that the Christian church in Canada will continue to hold forth the word of life and that God may be pleased to pour out his Spirit on us in these days. To God be the glory forever.

"Whoever has ears, let them hear what the Spirit says to the church" (Rev. 2:7, 11, 17, 29; 3:6, 13, 22).

4

CHURCH AND STATE: THEOLOGICAL PERSPECTIVES

Stephen J. Wellum

As Canadians and Christians, the year 2017 marke two noteworthy anniversaries: the 150th anniversary of Canada as a nation and the 90th anniversary of Toronto Baptist Seminary in training men and women for gospel ministry. In thinking about the relationship between the two anniversaries, namely the state and the seminary as an arm of the church, it is unquestionable that the impact of the Christian worldview on Canadian history is significant.[1] In fact, it is nigh impossible to recount the last 150 years without thinking about the unique social, political, and economic impact the church has had on Canada.

What is true of Canadian history is also true of Western European history. Although the European Union tried to recount its history apart from the impact of Christianity, this is a hopeless task.[2] The Western world and the freedoms she has enjoyed is impossible to understand apart from the impact of the gospel in Europe, specifically the theological influence of the Reformation

---

[1] On this point, see Chapter 1: Sit Lux: Evangelicalism in Ontario 1790's–1890's, and Chapter 2: A Century of Change: Protestantism in Canada in the Twentieth Century.

[2] On the European Union's attempt to do so, see George Weigel, *The Cube and the Cathedral: Europe, America, and Politics Without God* (New York: Basic Books, 2005).

on the larger social, cultural, economic, and political structures of the West.[3]

Years ago, Francis Schaeffer used to speak of the twofold effect of the gospel on individuals *and* the larger society.[4] First, there is the *primary* effect that results in the triune God bringing new life to individuals by regeneration, justification, and placing them in local churches that faithfully preach and live out the gospel. Second, there is the *secondary* effect of the gospel that benefits the larger society due to God's common grace and the salt and light effect of the church. Regarding the second effect, this does *not* entail that the entire nation is "Christian;" instead it means that the nation was affected by Christian truth and values that impacted the nation. For example, due to the influence of Christianity on Canada (and other Western nations), even among unbelievers, there was an acceptance and endorsement of Christian values such as the sanctity and protection of human life, the preservation of human rights, and the guarding of marriage and the family—all values that are the direct result of Christianity's impact on the culture in contrast to other worldview perspectives. In fact, where the impact of Christianity has been experienced in nations, Schaeffer argued that these nations established a "form" to their society; namely, a rule of law that was broadly Christian, and within that "form," these countries experienced unparalleled "freedoms" in contrast to other nations not impacted by Christianity. However, as the "form" of Christianity is rejected and replaced by other worldview alternatives such as secularism or other religious perspectives, not

---

[3] For a defense of this point, see David W. Hall, *Calvin in the Public Square: Liberal Democracies, Rights, and Civil Liberties* (Phillipsburg, NJ: P&R, 2009).

[4] For example, see Francis A. Schaeffer, *A Christian Manifesto* (Wheaton, IL: Crossway, 2005).

THEOLOGICAL PERSPECTIVES

only are the "form" and "laws" redefined, but the "freedoms" that people once enjoyed are also undermined. In the case of the Western world, Schaeffer predicted that only so many options faced countries in this situation, and his greatest fear was the rise of "statism," which always demands our total allegiance to Caesar without compromise. What Schaeffer observed many years ago has been confirmed in the West as we have witnessed an increasing move to eliminate Christian thought and values from the society and to squelch all dissent. But with that said, as we reflect on the last 150 years of Canadian history, Christians ought to thank God for Canada—a nation that has experienced unparalleled freedoms largely due to the impact of the gospel. What the future holds for Canada is unknown, but Christians are right to thank God for Canada despite her shortcomings.

However, much has changed, especially in the last fifty years, and much of the change is not for the better, contra the arguments of some. For example, on July 1, 2016, John Stackhouse wrote a provocative piece entitled "Canada: Getting Worse—and Better."[5] In the article, Stackhouse responds to various doomsayers who lament the loss of Christian influence in Canada and thus believe she is getting worse. In the post, he tries to convince Canadian Christians that, despite the loss of Christian influence in the country, Canada really is better off than it was a century ago. To prove his point, he compares what Canada was like in 1916 to 2016 by employing his understanding of "biblical standards of justice and compassion." In his analysis he admits that today's church attendance is much less than it was in 1916, where two-thirds of Canadians attended church services, compared to less than two percent today. He also

---

[5] "Canada: Getting Worse—and Better" johnstackhouse.com/2016/07/01/canada-getting-worse-and-better/ (accessed October 3, 2018).

acknowledges that in 1916 politicians would consult the advice of various church leaders, Sunday was reserved for the Lord's Day, and in our public schools the Lord's Prayer was recited. But in a strange twist of logic, Stackhouse thinks that although the "Christian" nature of the country has dramatically decreased, we are in a *better* situation now if we compare how Canada treats women, the poor, and homosexuals to their treatment in 1916. No doubt there is truth in what Stackhouse is saying following his criteria of justice and compassion, but the problem is that his analysis is woefully inadequate in terms of a full-orbed biblical standard. Nowhere does he analyze the erosion that has occurred in Canada due to a rejection of Christianity regarding such foundational moral issues as the treatment of the unborn, the protection and valuing of marriage and the family, the protection of the aged, and other societal signs of decay such as the rise of pornography, suicide, drugs, and so on. Why are these fundamental values of Scripture tied to creation order absent in Stackhouse's analysis?

With all due respect to Stackhouse, in every measure, Canada has dramatically changed, and it is *not* for the better. On every side, we are not only seeing the collapse of Christianity's influence in the culture, but also the attempt to dismantle any Christian influence root and branch. It is hardly accidental that a "common morality" that kept Canada together is now disappearing at an alarming rate. With the breakdown of the most foundational units in society such as marriage and the family, along with a trivialization of human life, we are now witnessing the disastrous social, economic, and political consequences that are shaking the foundations of Canadian society. Given these seismic changes, I am not sure what another 150 years will bring apart from God's sovereign grace in seeing the gospel transform people in the twofold way that Schaeffer describes. It is simply naïve to think that Canada can continue on her present course and maintain the freedoms and privileges she has previously enjoyed. Our present course will inevitably lead to internal social, political, and economic collapse. History also bears witness to this truth. In many ways, our current context is parallel to Augustine's situation living on the precipice of the collapse of the Western portion of the Roman Empire. As he wrote in his famous book *The City of God*,[6] nations come and go, including the nation of Canada, and it is only the church that remains forever.

In this context, then, what does "desiring a better country" mean as we look forward? As Christians, what should we think about Canada as a nation and her future? Is our aim to make Canada more Christian by trying to return to the good old days? Is our energy and time to be spent seeing the Bible verses quoted in our "Coat of Arms" realized? For example, is it our aim to see Canada acknowledge that "God shall have dominion from sea to sea" as picked up in the phrase "From sea to sea" taken from Psalm 72:8? Is "Desiring a better country" our aim, a phrase taken from Hebrews 11:6? In fact, do these verses in our Coat of Arms even refer to Canada? All of these questions demand careful biblical and theological reflection. In truth, all of these questions centre on the larger question of the Church-State relationship. What exactly is this relationship, biblically speaking? And where does Toronto Baptist Seminary fit in this discussion as a theological institution functioning as an arm of the church and called to train men and women for gospel ministry?

Given the occasion of our celebration of the two anniversaries, the goal of this article is to answer some of these questions by reflecting on the Church-State relationship. My aim is to give some biblical-theological clarity about how we as Christians and

---

[6] Augustine, *City of God* (trans. Henry Bettenson; New York: Penguin, reprint, 2004).

Canadians should think about our nation and our role as the church living in Canada as we face an uncertain future. Given the enormity of these issues, I can only briefly discuss these matters and I will do so in three steps: First, I will begin by making an initial observation about "desiring a better country" and the texts used in the "Coat of Arms" regarding their biblical fidelity. Second, I will sketch how the Church-State relationship is presented and developed in Scripture. Third, I will conclude with some applications as we seek to live as the church in Canada now and in the years ahead.

An Initial Observation about the Use of Scripture in "Desiring a Better Country"

"Desiring a better country" is found in Canada's Coat of Arms, which also includes the phrase, from "sea to sea." These phrases are drawn from Scripture with the former from Hebrews 11:16 and the latter from Psalm 72:8. These phrases not only reflect Christianity's influence on Canada, but also a problem, namely the misuse of Scripture as applied to Canada as a nation. In their contexts, Hebrews 11:16 and Psalm 72:8 do not mean what they mean in the Coat of Arms.

Psalm 72 is a statement about the Davidic king tied to the promises of the Davidic Covenant inaugurated in 2 Samuel 7. When Psalm 72 is placed in the Psalter and its redemptive-historical location in the Old Testament, it is ultimately a promise of the coming of David's greater Son, our Lord Jesus Christ, which is also tied to the Prophetic anticipation of the dawning of the New Covenant, the establishment of the church, and the victory of our Lord in his cross and resurrection as he inaugurates the dawning of the new creation. In truth, this text does *not* apply to Canada as a nation or any nation. As I will argue below, Canada cannot be viewed as a "new Israel" with a Davidic king

Theological Perspectives

ruling over her, nor is she the church. In God's plan, nations are important and they serve their role. In fact, governments are ordained by God to serve a vital purpose (Rom. 13:1-7), but Canada is *not* the fulfillment of this text. The same is true of Hebrews 11:16, which refers to the Christian's desire and longing for the consummated state of the new creation, not a better Canadian nation. The use of these texts reflects an improper association of the church with the state, something that is also not uncommon in the use of these texts in European and American history. No doubt, the use of these texts reflects the impact of the gospel on western nations, which has yielded many positive results, but also some negative ones, specifically the idea of a "civil religion" with its attending problems. Biblically, we cannot link the church and state this way. As Christians, we thank God for the privilege of living in Canada with its rich heritage, but also, we must exercise caution in thinking of Canada as a "Christian nation," something the use of these texts implies. As the church, we have responsibilities to our nation, but we must never confuse the church with the state. How, then, should we think about the Church-State relationship? It is to this question that we now turn.

The Church-State Relationship: Biblical-Theological Reflections

What is the relationship between the church and the state? In theology, there has been a tendency to identify too quickly Israel as a nation with our nations today, which is implicitly reflected in our Coat of Arms. To answer this question, we must follow the Bible's own presentation of these concepts from creation to new creation and pay careful attention to the progression of the biblical covenants, starting with Adam as the covenant head of the old creation and moving to our Lord Jesus Christ as the head of the New Covenant. It is only when we do this that we will be able to capture how Scripture presents the Church-State relationship, and thus form proper applications for us today.[7]

Creation & the Creation Covenant (Genesis 1-2, 3-5)

The Bible's story begins in creation with the glory of the eternal triune God. As the Creator, God is the sovereign King and he rules over all. Also, given who God is, he has the moral authority and right to rule all things; God's rule is total. In creation, then, due to who God is as our Creator and who we are as his creatures, there is no distinction between public and private spheres, or the sacred and secular. Also, due to our creation in God's image, God authorizes humans to rule over his creation as his image-sons and representative rulers (Gen. 1:26-31; cf. Psalm 8). There is no higher calling placed on humans, who are created to be in covenant relationship with our Creator and, under his sovereign Lordship, to rule as his vice-regents as kings and queens.[8]

In creation, we also discover that the central building block of all human societies is marriage and the family (Genesis 2). Societies arise out of marriage and the family, which also leads to the creation grounding for the idea of government. Why? Because as a result of marriage and the family, and in order to fulfill God's purpose to rule over creation as his covenant image-sons and representatives, we need order, organization, and the employment of our God-given gifts and abilities to see Eden's borders expanded to the uttermost parts of the earth.[9] Though

---

[7] For a more detailed discussion of this approach, see Peter J. Gentry and Stephen J. Wellum, *Kingdom through Covenant: A Biblical-Theological Understanding of the Covenants*, 2nd ed. (Wheaton, IL: Crossway, 2018).

[8] For a discussion of each of these points, see Gentry and Wellum, *Kingdom through Covenant*, 211-258, 666-685.

[9] See Gentry and Wellum, *Kingdom through Covenant*, 211-258.

human authority is always derivative and contingent, we were created to rule, and government is part of how humans fulfill their calling as image-sons in relation to God. From the very beginning, God's kingdom and rule comes through humans in covenant relationship to God and to one another.[10] The biblical basis, then, for the state and the role of human government is grounded in creation; it is not the result of a fallen order.

Yet, with that said, the entrance of sin into the world in Genesis 3 changes everything. Sin, at its heart, is human rebellion and revolt against the rule and glory of God (Rom. 3:23). Sin does not diminish God's sovereign rule over this world. After all, God is the triune Creator and Lord and his rule is universal, total, and absolute. As Abraham Kuyper famously stated many years ago, "There is not a square inch in the whole domain of our human existence over which Christ, who is Sovereign over all, does not cry, 'Mine!'"[11] However, since the Fall, God's rule has been foolishly contested. Though humans are still made in the image of God, they now reflect a distorted image and rule. Thankfully, due to a saving promise (Gen. 3:15), God has not left us to ourselves, but has chosen by sovereign grace to restore our vice-regency by another Adam—a better, last Adam—which is the glorious plan of redemption that unfolds across redemptive history.

However, the Fall does create two humanities: one humanity, by God's grace, that stands in covenant relationship with God, and the other humanity who stands in opposition to God's rule and reign. We can even say that these two humanities are

---

[10] Some people question whether there is a creation covenant established in Genesis 1-3. For a defense of a creation covenant, see Gentry and Wellum, *Kingdom through Covenant*, 211-258, 666-685.

[11] James D. Bratt, ed., *Abraham Kuyper: A Centennial Reader* (Grand Rapids, MI: Eerdmans, 1998), 488.

two kingdoms, but we need to exercise care and *not* think that God is only King over one of the kingdoms. God is still the sovereign Lord over his entire creation regardless of our relationship to him, and he demands from us complete obedience and worship. Yet, with this caveat, it is correct to say that in light of the Fall, we can make a distinction between the sovereign rule of God over the entire creation and the "coming" of his saving reign in the context of a rebellious creation, to make all things right. God's kingdom "coming" does not mean that God gains rule where he did not have it before. Instead, it means that his rule is now named, acknowledged, executed and made visible, which is precisely what occurs through the unfolding of the biblical covenants.[12]

In summary, the creation that was originally created good (Gen. 1:31) has now become corrupt due to Adam's sin (Gen. 3; cf. Rom. 5:12-21). If God chooses to make things right, he, as the Lord, must initiate to save (which is how the Bible's redemptive storyline unfolds). In order to set creation right, God must act in salvation and judgment, provide a Redeemer who will usher in a new creation by paying for our sin and defeating death, and create a new creation—a city whose builder and maker is God, the home of righteousness (2 Peter 3:13). In fact, this city is what Hebrews is talking about when it refers to "desiring a better country" (Heb. 11:16). The country spoken about is the result of God's sovereign, redemptive action through Christ in the establishment of a new creation and a heavenly Jerusalem; it is not identified with any earthly nation. Eventually, when all sin and evil is destroyed, we will see the establishment of a new creation, in contrast to what was lost in the old creation due to Adam's sin and rebellion.

---

[12] On this point, see Gentry and Wellum, *Kingdom through Covenant*, 648-654.

THEOLOGICAL PERSPECTIVES

The Noahic Covenant (Genesis 6-9)[13]

What is the context of the Noahic Covenant (Genesis 6-9)? It is this: God continues to rule as King over all creation, but in light of Genesis 3, human rebellion foolishly contests God's rule. In fact, human sin is so bad that God executes judgment on the entire human race by a universal flood, except for one man and his family—a display of divine judgment and sovereign grace.

After the Flood, God formalizes a covenant with Noah (Gen. 6:8, 18; 9:9-17). God's promise is that the divine intention of creation will not be lost. God solemnly promises that humanity's creational mandate (cf. 9:1-7; 1:26-30) will never again be interrupted by a suspension of the natural order like the Flood. The earth will be inhabited with life, and humans will continue to know the Lord through a covenant relationship. In the Noahic covenant, there is the anticipation of a "new creation," that is, a reversal of sin and death, especially linked to the promise of Genesis 3:15. The covenant is described as "everlasting," which is defined "as long as the earth endures" (8:22), meaning until the end of time and until the consummation of all things.

What is the significance of the Noahic covenant for our discussion? Let us note a number of key points. First, the Noahic covenant reminds us that two humanities or two kingdoms will continue until the consummation. Fallen humanity will simultaneously exist alongside God's people until the end. Second, in terms of the significance of the Noahic Covenant for our understanding of the state and the kingdoms of this world, it is best to think of the Noahic Covenant as a "common covenant" tied to creation.[14] In this covenant, because God is the sovereign

---

[13] For a detailed discussion of the Noahic covenant, see Gentry and Wellum, *Kingdom through Covenant*, 179-209.

[14] The distinction between "common covenants" and "special covenants" is from Jonathan Leeman, *How the Nations Rage: Rethinking*

Creator and Lord, he still commands and demands that all people without exception worship and obey him. Whether God's Lordship is recognized or not, he rules over all people, and eventually what results from Noah is the existence of all nations (see Genesis 10). All nations and peoples are accountable to their Creator and Lord.

Third, the Noahic covenant continues creation order and structures that are universal and normative for all societies. For example, the sanctity of human life is maintained (see Gen. 9:6), along with marriage and the family as the basic unit of society. We also see the continued institution of the state that continues from creation but now in the context of a fallen order. In fact, God authorizes the state to rule and execute judgment (see Gen. 9:6), just as he authorizes parents to rule in the family. God authorizes the state to bear the sword and to enact justice, which is now necessary due to the Fall. By the sign of the covenant, namely God's bow in the sky, God teaches us that he has temporarily laid his weapons down, although final judgment is coming.[15] Instead of executing final judgment immediately however, it will be delayed until all of God's redemptive purposes are achieved. In the meantime, the state is ordained to execute justice (Gen. 8:21; cf. Rom. 13:1-7), and all people are called to be God's subjects and citizens, although the kingdom of man continues to reject God's rule as evidenced in the Tower of Babel (Gen. 11).

Thus, under the Noahic Covenant, which is an extension of Adamic rule, the state, established in creation, continues to exercise rule and is given institutional expression but now in the context of a fallen world. Governments exist to provide a

---

Faith and Politics in a Divided Age (Nashville, TN: Thomas Nelson, 2018).

[15] See Gentry and Wellum, *Kingdom through Covenant*, 179-209.

platform for activity of Adamic citizenship, which is primarily concerned with sustaining and protecting human life and preserving an orderly and just society so that humans can live and act.

But given human sin, God also establishes a series of "special covenants," namely the Abrahamic, Mosaic, Davidic, and the New Covenant, to keep and fulfill his initial saving promise (Gen. 3:15) and to redeem and undo Adam's disastrous choice. In these covenants, God elects a people who are called to embody his rule, modeling what God intended for all humanity in creation. Special covenants serve the purpose of the common covenants by fulfilling them. What the common covenants command, the special covenants provide. God's rule through covenant relationship is revealed and it is to be visibly acknowledged.

The Abrahamic Covenant (Genesis 12, 15, 17, 22)[16]

The Abrahamic Covenant is a special covenant that stands in contrast to the judgments of God on human sin and presents anew the plan of creation. Given its location in the Bible's storyline, it is God's response to Genesis 3-11 and is tied to God's sovereign grace and initiative to elect and redeem.

Important elements from creation are repeated in the blessing to Abraham: God's promise of a great name and seed, the multiplication of humans, the provision of the land, a peaceful relationship between God and humanity, and the restoration of the nations (Gen. 12:1-3; cf. 15:4-5; 17:1-8; 18:18-19; 22:16-18). Yet, unlike what happens with Noah, God does not destroy the human race and re-boot it again. Instead, God allows the nations to exist and then calls Abraham out of the nations to become a great nation (*gôy*)—a world political community and a

---

[16] On the Abrahamic covenant, see Gentry and Wellum, *Kingdom through Covenant*, 259-337, 687-694.

kingdom in the full political sense of the word. In Abraham we have a recovery of the divine goal for creation and humans, namely, the restoration of God's rule and reign over this world, albeit imperfectly. Abraham and his offspring exist side-by-side with the nations, who are also commanded to serve, obey, and worship their Creator.

God's intent is to work through Abraham and his seed to bring blessing to the nations and to make Abraham a great "nation." It is best to view the Abrahamic Covenant as the means by which God will fulfill his promises for humanity first promised in Genesis 3:15 through the provision of a greater Adam (cf. Gal 3:16). In Abraham and his seed, first in Isaac, then in corporate Israel, and then in an individual Davidic king, all of God's promises for the human race will be enacted—promises that God will unilaterally accomplish (see Genesis 15).

Abraham and the subsequent nation of Israel are to visibly demonstrate "kingdom through covenant." They are to be a visible expression of Adam's role as image-son and priest-king. They are to display God's own character and rule and do what is just and right (Gen. 18:19). In Abraham and his seed, God will fulfill the role he created humans to have.

Yet unless God unilaterally acts to keep his promise, there is no hope in Abraham alone. In this sense, the Abrahamic Covenant is also prophetic. Abraham and his seed are called to be image-sons and priest-kings, but for that to take place, God will have to act by the provision of a son greater than Isaac (see Genesis 22). Why? Because we need a person from the human race and from Abraham's line who will ultimately obey for us and bear our sin before God.

THEOLOGICAL PERSPECTIVES

The Old Covenant (Exodus 19-20, Pentateuch)[17]

The "Old Covenant," or Israel's covenant mediated through Moses, is grounded in the promises to the patriarchs. It is as the God of Abraham, Isaac, and Jacob that God calls Moses to deliver his people from Egypt (Ex. 3:6; cf. 2:24-25; Deut. 4:36-38; 1 Chron. 16:15-19; 2 Kings 13:22-23). God did not set his love on Israel because they were better or more numerous than the nations (Deut. 7:7). Neither was it for their righteousness that they were given the land of Canaan. The basis for God's calling of Israel was not to be found in them, but in God's grace and his covenant loyalty to his promises to Abraham, Isaac, and Jacob (Ex. 19:4; Deut. 7:8).

In the Old Covenant, God's plan is to bring blessing to all nations and ultimately restore creation in and through the nation of Israel. Israel as a nation is the agent and means God uses to achieve the wider purposes of the Abrahamic Covenant tied to God's initial promise in Genesis 3:15. In this regard, Exodus 19:5-6 is an important description of Israel. God calls Israel, the corporate expression of Abraham's seed, "my possession," a "kingdom of priests," and a "holy nation" (*gôy*). Building on the previous covenant promises, Israel is presented as the means by which the Abrahamic promise is fulfilled. The nation is distinguished from the rest of the nations to reflect visibly what God's kingdom is to look like through covenant relationship with him. This is why Israel is to function as the paradigm of theocratic rule. Israel is the agent God uses to achieve the wider purposes of the Abrahamic Covenant, which is ultimately bound up with the redemption of the entire world (Gen. 12:1-3).

This truth is confirmed by a further description of Israel's relationship to the Lord, namely a Father-son relationship (Ex.

---

[17] On the Old Covenant, see Gentry and Wellum, *Kingdom through Covenant*, 339-442, 694-700.

4:22-23). This description goes back to Adam, who is the first image-son and representative of God (see Luke 3:38). It also looks forward to the rise of the Davidic kings, who are the individual expression of what Israel as a nation is called to be, namely God's son. Just as God demands perfect obedience from his creatures, so he demands the same from his covenant people. Yet, like Adam, Israel repeatedly disobeys and judgment falls on them. Israel does not visibly demonstrate "kingdom through covenant." They fail to serve as the model nation to the nations. Sadly, despite her privileges, Israel looks a lot like the surrounding nations (see the book of Judges). Circumcision, the sign of the covenant that signified priestly devotion, was only true of them outwardly but not inwardly. Israel, as a microcosm of the human race, needs a true circumcision of the heart and the forgiveness of her sin to be a true covenant-keeper and faithful to the God of creation and redemption.

However, it is also crucial to see that the Old Covenant not only exposed the sin and failure of Israel, it was also prophetic, thus pointing forward to the need for a greater "Israel" and a truly obedient "Son." Within the Old Covenant, God gives a number of typological patterns that anticipate how he is going to keep his promises. All of those patterns reach their fulfillment first in Christ. For example, Israel functions as a "kingdom of priests" who are to be fully devoted to their covenant Lord and dwell before him, yet in their sin they need "priests" to act on their behalf to deal with their sin before God (Heb. 5:1; 7:11). In fact, the entire sacrificial system points to the need for a greater sacrifice and a greater priest to come (Ex. 25:9, 40; Hebrews 8–9), which is fulfilled in Christ and his work. Or, think how the Exodus becomes an entire pattern and typological structure that anticipates a greater exodus/redemption to come, ultimately fulfilled in Christ (Ex. 15:14-17; Isa. 11:15-16; 40:3-5; 41:17-20;

42:14-16; 48:20-21; 49:8-12; 51:9-11; 52:3-6, 11-12; 55:12-13; Hos. 11:1; 13:4-5). Or, Moses in so many ways anticipates a greater Moses to come (Deut. 18:15-18; Num. 12:1-8; Deut. 34:10-12; Acts 3:17-26). Or, within the Old Covenant is the anticipation of a coming king which points forward to the Davidic king and its ultimate fulfillment in Christ (Deut. 17:14-20; cf. Gen. 17:6, 16; 49:8-12; Num. 24:17-19; cf. 24:7; Joshua-Judges; cf. Josh. 23:1-16; Judges 2:16-3:6; 9:1-57).

What is the significance of the Old Covenant for our understanding of the Church-State relationship? One crucial point is that we must exercise care in moving too quickly from Israel to other nations and countries, like Canada. This point has often been violated in theology. Israel is *not* exactly like the other nations. In God's plan, Israel is God's chosen people to visibly represent what the nations do not. They are constituted as a theocratic nation (Ex. 19:6) to reveal God to the nations as sons, and through them to usher in God's saving reign to this world (cf. Gen. 12:1-3). As such, we cannot directly apply nation of Israel texts to Canada or any other nation. Furthermore, in the Bible's storyline, Israel functions to reveal the problem of the human heart. Like the nations, and despite her privileges, Israel disobeys. Israel as a nation demonstrates that she is not a faithful covenant-keeper. Israel is a disobedient son and a failed kingdom of priests—just like Adam. Israel as a nation is to be light to the nations, but they too need a Redeemer. This does not entail that there was no believing remnant within the nation, but it does mean that as a corporate people, Israel breaks the covenant and points forward to the need for a faithful Israelite, uniquely expressed in the Davidic king.

The Davidic Covenant (2 Samuel 7)[18]

In the Bible's storyline, the Davidic Covenant is the epitome of the Old Testament covenants because it brings the previous covenants to their climax in the king. In the Davidic king is found the hope of the world, yet this hope is never realized; it is only anticipated in a greater David to come who will be the perfect covenant-keeper and fulfill all of God's promises.

The Davidic Covenant consists of two main parts: first, God's promises about the establishment of David's house forever (2 Sam. 7:12-16), and second, the promises concerning the "Father-son" relationship between God and the Davidic king (2 Sam. 7:14; cf. Ps. 2; 89:26-27). In this context, "sonship" is significant because it inextricably ties the Davidic Covenant to the previous covenants, and it also anticipates in type the greater Sonship of Christ. Regarding the former, the sonship applied to corporate Israel (Ex. 4:22-23; cf. Hos. 11:1) now is applied to the individual Davidic king, who, in himself, is the "true Israel." In the Davidic king, corporate Israel has been reduced to an individual who will accomplish all of God's saving purposes. The Davidic king becomes the administrator and mediator of the covenant, thus representing God's rule to the people and representing the people as a whole (2 Sam. 7:22-24). The Davidic king also fulfills the role of Adam; it is through the king that God's rule is enacted in the world (2 Sam. 7:19b). This is not surprising if we link the covenants together by carefully following their progression from creation to David. Since at the centre of God's redemptive plan is the restoration of humanity's vice-regent role in creation through a human seed, by the time we get to David, we now know it is through the king that creation will be restored. In the Old Testament, this truth is borne out in many places,

---

[18] On the Davidic Covenant, see Gentry and Wellum, *Kingdom through Covenant*, 443-485, 700-704.

especially the Psalter, which envisions the Davidic son as executing a universal rule (e.g., Ps. 2, 8, 45, 72, cf. Isa. 9:6-7, 11, 53).

However, in Old Testament history, there is a major problem that creates a question as to how God is going to fulfill his promises. Similar to previous covenant mediators, the Davidic kings disobey and come under God's judgment, yet the hope of the redemption depends on them. God continues in his unilateral determination to keep his promise to bring forth the seed of Abraham, now more specifically a Davidic king, who will reign over the whole world. And yet, there is no faithful king-son who effects God's kingdom or saving reign. This leads to the message of the prophets and the anticipation of a New Covenant.

The Prophets & the Expectation of a New Covenant[19]

The Old Testament writing prophets are covenantally located post-Davidic. This is significant because their prophecies build on what God has already revealed through the previous covenants, which find their epitome in the Davidic Covenant. The prophets not only speak of God's judgment upon the nation for their violation of the covenant, but they also proclaim an overall pattern of renewal by recapitulating the past history of redemption and projecting it into the future.[20] The prophets announce that unless God saves his people there is no hope. God must act to save or there will be no salvation at all.

But alongside the truth that the Lord must save his people is the emphasis that God must do so through a faithful Davidic

---

[19] On the prophetic teaching of the New Covenant, see Gentry and Wellum, *Kingdom through Covenant*, 487-643.

[20] On this point, see Graeme Goldsworthy, *According to Plan: The Unfolding Revelation of God in the Bible* (Downers Grove, IL: IVP Academic, 2013).

king (Isa. 7:14; 9:6-7; 11:1-10; 42:1-9; 49:1-7; 52:13-53:12; 55:3; 61:1-3; Jer. 23:5-6; 33:14-26; Ezek. 34:23-24; 37:24-28). In this king, identified as the "servant of the Lord," a new or everlasting covenant will come, and with it the outpouring of the Spirit (Ezek. 36:24-38; 37:11-28; Joel 2:28-32), the forgiveness of sin (Jer. 31:34), and the dawning of a new creation (Isa. 65:17). The hope of the prophets is found in the New Covenant.[21]

Within the Old Testament, the New Covenant is viewed as national and international (Jer. 31:31-40; 33:6-16; Ezek. 36:24-38; 37:11-28). As a result of God's salvation through the Davidic king, a new people will be created that will truly and visibly be what God created his image-bearers to be. It will include Jews and Gentiles, and its scope will be universal, thus fulfilling the Abrahamic promise (Isa. 14:1-2; 19:23-25; 42:6, 20; 49:6; 55:3-5; 56:4-8; 66:18-24; Jer. 16:19; 33:9; Ezek. 36:36; 37:28; Amos 9:11-12; cf. Ps. 47:9; 87:3-6; 67:2-3; 117:1). Isaiah projects the ultimate fulfillment of the divine promises in the New Covenant onto an "ideal Israel," namely, a people united to the Servant located in a rejuvenated new creation (Isa. 65:17; 66:22). This "ideal Israel" picks up the promises to Abraham and is the ultimate fulfillment of the covenants that God established with Adam, the patriarchs, Israel, and David's son.

What is "new" about the New Covenant? Given space limitations, we will answer this question from one significant New Covenant text: Jeremiah 31:29-34. This text defines "newness" by a change in the structure and nature of God's people because of the work of its greater covenant mediator. Let us look at these respective changes.

First, the New Covenant changes the *structure* of God's people. Under the Old Covenant, God dealt with his people in a

---

[21] On this point, see Gentry and Wellum, *Kingdom through Covenant*, 704-712.

mediated or "tribal-representative" structure, whereby God related to them through specially-called mediators. The Old Testament does pay attention to individual believers, as evidenced in the remnant theme. But in general, the people's knowledge of God and their relationship with him depended upon specially-endowed leaders. The entire nation benefited when these leaders did right, and they suffered when they did not. Thus, the Old Testament does not emphasize God's Spirit being poured out on every individual believer and empowering them, but rather it is bestowed distinctively on prophets, priests, kings, and other designated leaders. But Jeremiah signals a structural shift in the covenant community where *all* of God's people will know him, from the least to the greatest. By this change, the New Covenant raises *every member* of the covenant to the same relationship with God through the universal distribution of the Spirit (see Joel 2:28-32; Acts 2). The Messiah, being the first to be anointed with the Spirit (see Isa. 11:1-3; 49:1-2; 61:1ff), will in turn pour out his Spirit on all flesh, namely, everyone within the covenant community (see Ezek. 11:19-20; 36:25-27; Joel 2:28-32; cf. Num. 11:27-29).

Second, the New Covenant changes the *nature* of God's people. Jeremiah distinguishes between the Old and the New Covenant based on the heart condition of its members (Jer. 31:31-34). Whereas only a remnant under the Old Covenant truly knew the Lord, God changes the heart of every New Covenant member: "I will write [my law] on their hearts... And no longer shall each one teach his neighbor ... for they shall all know me, from the least of them to the greatest, declares the LORD" (Jer. 31:33-34). Describing the law as written on the heart mirrors "circumcision of the heart" (cf. Deut. 30:6; cf. Deut. 10:16; Jer. 4:4; 9:25), closely tied to regeneration (Rom. 2:29). This does not entail that there were no regenerate Old Testament saints, but it does imply that the new people will all be regenerate, which is a major change. The Old Covenant community was a mixed people (Rom. 9:6), but this is not true of the New. The entire community will know God and obey from the heart because of the Spirit's work.

Third, the New Covenant changes the *sacrifice* made for God's people. The Old Covenant offered the forgiveness of sins through the priestly-sacrificial system. But "it is impossible for the blood of bulls and goats to take away sins" (Heb. 10:4). The Old Covenant sacrifices were designed to remind God's covenant people of their sinfulness through repetition. Yet, Jeremiah says that in the New Covenant, tied to its glorious mediator, God "will remember their sins and their lawless deeds no more" (Jer. 31:33–34; Heb. 10:17). In the Old Testament, "remembering" is not simple recall (cf. Gen. 8:1; 1 Sam. 1:19). That God "will remember their sins no more" implies that under the New Covenant a better priest will offer a better sacrifice (Ps. 110) and that all in the covenant will experience the complete forgiveness of sins. This is at the heart of the New Covenant, answering our need.

Christ and the New Covenant[22]

Our Lord Jesus Christ fulfills the expectation and promises of the Old Testament in his first coming, at least in an inaugurated form, which will reach its consummation at his return. Yet, *all* that the Old Testament anticipated is now here *in principle*, yet not in its fullness. In Jesus' cross alone is sin paid for, and death is destroyed in his glorious resurrection. In his obedient life and cross-work he has undone what Adam began (Heb. 2:5–18) and created a new people, namely the church, who now visibly

---

[22] For a detailed treatment of this section, see Gentry and Wellum, *Kingdom through Covenant*, 713–765.

display God's glory by beginning to fulfill her purpose as God's New Covenant people, the people of the new creation.

In thinking about the nature of the church, especially in relation to the state, it is crucial to note a number of truths. First, the church is *not* the same as Israel of old, given the fulfillment that has come in Christ. The church is *new* because of her identification with Christ; she is the people of the New Covenant and the beginning of the new creation. Second, the church cannot be identified with any nation or country. The church is the "age to come" community now living its life here on earth because of her union with Christ. The church's identity is *not* with "this present age" but with the saving reign of Christ that is now here. Those who have placed their faith in Christ are now citizens of the new, heavenly Jerusalem, transferred from being "in Adam" to being "in Christ." This is the point of Hebrews 12:18-29. In contrast with the Israelites who assembled at Sinai, as New Covenant believers we have already gathered to meet God at the "heavenly Jerusalem" (vv. 22-24). As the church, we are beginning to enjoy by faith the privileges of that city still to come (Heb. 13:14). None of these truths may be said of earthly nations that are completely identified with "this present age" and who are passing away. It is only the church that enters into the new creation, not the kingdoms and nations of this earth.

The church, then, given who she is, is called to visibly demonstrate what it means to be an image-bearer, priest-king, and son as God's New Covenant people. God calls us now to live out what we are by the work of the Spirit. In the church, our triune God has begun to restore what we were created to be in the first place. In the church, God's saving rule arrives and we are called to display to the world what covenant-keepers are to look like. Ultimately in the church, our destiny is to rule over the entire creation, but this still awaits the "not yet," although even now the church is to exercise the keys of the kingdom in her midst.

Edmund Clowney captures these truths well when he writes about what the church is:

> The church as the community of Christ's kingdom on earth is a theo-political order. While all things are under the rule of Christ, it is his saving rule that constitutes his kingdom (Col. 1:13). The church is the heavenly polis on earth, the new humanity whose hearts have been circumcised by the Holy Spirit. Its breadth reaches out to all peoples; its depth renews the heart (Jer. 32:39; Ezek. 11:19). We have no abiding city here; the church cannot be identified with the kingdoms of this world (Heb. 13:14). But we do have a city with foundations, whose builder and maker is God. As such, the church exercises heavenly citizenship in the fellowship of the saints (Heb. 11:10, 16; 12:28; Phil. 3:20). The community exists on earth, but is governed by the keys of the heavenly kingdom, with spiritual, not physical sanctions (Matt. 16:19; Rev. 3:7).[23]

In light of this reality, what is the church's mission? To answer this question, we need to think in terms of the *broad* and *narrow* mission of the church.[24] *Broadly*, as God's new creation, our calling is to image God in everything tied to the purpose of our creation. In Christ, we are being remade after his glorified humanity and thus created to be all that God intended us to be in the original creation, plus more. Thus, as Christ's disciples, we are being restored to the purpose of our creation. This entails

---

[23] Edmund P. Clowney, *The Church* (Downers Grove: InterVarsity Press, 1995), 189.

[24] On the mission of the church, I am indebted to the discussion in Leeman, *How the Nations Rage*.

that in our everyday life, at home, or at work, we are to demonstrate what God requires of each one of us.

But we must also speak of the *narrow* mission of the church. Our mission is to make disciples by the proclamation of the gospel (Matt. 28:18-20). As those who have the keys of the kingdom, we draw the line between holy and unholy (Matt. 16:13-20; 18:15-20). Our calling is to proclaim the gospel to the nations and in our local assemblies to mark off Christ's holy people through the ordinances of baptism and the Lord's Supper.

Furthermore, given the truth of inaugurated eschatology, there are some crucial points to remember as we think about the church's mission. In the present or the "already," Christ has paid for our sin and secured our justification, but until he returns, he does not lift the curse totally from creation. For us, the complete removal of sin and the curse and the establishment of the new creation await the consummation. This is why "a better country," namely the new creation as a place, is still future to us. Our Lord Jesus presently rules over every square inch as the King of kings, but at this moment the Genesis 3 curse is still with us. Until Christ returns, everything still dies. All of our work, politics, art, romance, and so on is still under the curse of this "present age" although we are participants of the "age to come." Christ's kingship is universal but it is not yet publicly acknowledged. It is only in Christ's people, the church, that Christ's lordship is acknowledged by the Spirit to the glory of God the Father. Although for the Christian there is no sacred and secular divide, there is still an unregenerate and regenerate divide until the end. This means that it is only the triune God who can regenerate and make alive by his transforming power. We, as Christians, are the beneficiaries of his work, but we cannot change or transform this world apart from the transforming work of God by the power of the preached Word.

A major implication of this truth in thinking about the church's mission is that Christians do not "redeem" creation or "transform" culture, contrary to the rhetoric of many today who call themselves "social justice warriors." We cannot redeem or transform anything, but we point to the triune God who alone can do so. God's kingdom comes to this world by his own sovereign initiative through the church that proclaims the glories of Christ. The primary mission of the church, then, is not to transform the world but to live together as a transformed people, and to invite the nations to Christ. The state continues to exercise her God-given authority until Christ's return, yet the church is not the state. The state belongs to the structures of this "present age" which are coming to their end, but the church is God's "age to come" people now living its life here as it awaits Christ's return. The church's mission is to live out what we are in Christ and to call all people to faith and repentance. When the mission of the church and the state are confused, we fail to grasp what God has intended for each institution in his overall plan, thus confusing the sphere God has intended for each one.

Theological Application
There is much that could be said in terms of application, but let me focus on first the state, the church, and then the place of Toronto Baptist Seminary in this discussion.

First, Christians are to think of the state, and specifically for our purposes, Canada, in terms of its God-ordained role, but also remember that ultimately all nations are passing away. If the Lord tarries, I do not know what another 150 years will bring for Canada but there is no guarantee that Canada will be around. Our hope is not to be found in Canada.

However, in the meantime, all nations, including Canada and her citizens, are called as God's creatures to submit to God's rule as their Creator and Lord. If nations and people within the nation do not, God will eventually bring judgment to both. God has established the state as a legitimate authority until the end, but given the abnormality of this present age, the state is only a faint reflection of what she should have been in the original creation. Yet, even as a fallen institution, God has ordained that the state exercise authority to uphold what is good and to punish evil according to God's creation standards. As Christians, it is our responsibility to call nations, including Canada, to their God-ordained role; to establish just and righteous governance that upholds the sanctity of human life in all of life, marriage, and the family unit. Why? Because this is part of creation order that God has established and we ignore or deny it to our peril. Furthermore, the state should also encourage and maintain the best environment where humans can flourish in their calling as image-bearers, which given the depravity of the human heart, implies a limited, yet important role for government.

In a fallen world, not all forms of government are equal; some fulfill God's ordained role for the state better than others. Given the corrosive effects of sin, many nations do not preserve what is just, but rather encourage what is unjust. Until King Jesus returns and brings this present age to its end, some nations will serve people in more just ways, while others will not. As Christians, we should encourage forms of government that preserve what is just and good. What form of government is this? Historically, one can make the case that nations influenced by the secondary effects of the gospel have been much more humane and just, despite their glaring imperfections. Nations that have encouraged the sanctity of life, marriage, and the family, private property, work, and the opportunity for human flourishing fulfill their intended purpose better than nations who do not. But it is a given that for nations who depart from the influence of the Christian worldview, tyranny is not far behind. This should be a sober lesson for nations such as Canada who have benefited from the secondary blessings of the gospel but now are determined to eradicate the influence of Christian truth and values from the nation's governance.

However, ultimately, as Christians, we know that we will only have a "better country" when Christ returns. In the meantime, the hope for Canada is not merely in legislating better laws, but for individuals within the nation to be made alive by the Spirit and for the church to have a salt and light influence on the larger society. It is only when the human heart is transformed by God's Spirit that we learn to love God and our neighbour—which is foundational for a just and humane society. No nation will achieve this result; this is only the result of God's gracious work through the church by the proclamation of the gospel. Apart from the primary and secondary effects of the gospel affecting Canada, realistically there is little hope for Canada to enjoy the freedoms and blessings she has enjoyed over the last 150 years.

Second, in terms of the church, we must never undervalue her significance and role in the world. In a day of "social justice warriors," who seem more determined to wed themselves to the "power" of the state and crave for the world's recognition, we must avoid this like the plague. The church is God's New Covenant people, joining Jew and Gentiles together as one new man, and thus we are the beginning of the new creation (Eph. 2:11-22). The church, as Christ's people, is the institution that alone lasts forever, and it is only in the church that the transformation of peoples takes place (Eph. 3:7-13). As our Lord taught us, the church is the people he has come to build and "the gates of Hades will not overcome it" (Matt. 16:18). Unlike the state, the church is identified with Christ and the "age to come" and it will never fade away. People only enter the church by regeneration, repentance, and faith in Christ. The church is not another human institution that merely does good work in the world. Instead, the church is an outpost of heaven and it consists of those who have entered God's kingdom by grace through faith in Christ alone.

The church alone does "kingdom" work, not the state. The state might legislate and try to curb human sin with limited success, but it is in the church that God's Word is preached and that people are given resurrection life. We think too highly of the power of Ottawa to bring change to Canada. It is only the church by the preached gospel that truly does kingdom work. The church's authority, then, is not found in wielding the authority of the state or by taking up this or that social cause. The church is strongest when she fulfills her calling to be what she is, namely, God's new creation people. The church does this depending on God's might and power by his Spirit through the preaching of his Word. It is God alone who can transform the human heart and he does so by his Word and Spirit. The church, through her offices of elders and deacons in conjunction with the entire people, is to act like God's New Covenant people by making disciples, exercising discipline, practicing the ordinances, and making visible to the world what redeemed, reconciled covenant-keepers look like. In this way, the church is called to bear witness to the nations the good news of salvation in Christ.

Furthermore, just as the state is to function within her God-ordained sphere, so the church is to function within her sphere. The church is an embassy of Christ's kingdom, representing the authority of Christ to the nations. By Christ's own authority, we are to be subject to the state (Mark 12:13-17; Rom. 13:1-2; Tit. 3:1), but Christian obedience to the state is never blind or total. The state is authorized by God to uphold justice and to punish evil, but this does not guarantee that she will do so well (see

Revelation 13-14). When the state commands what God forbids, or forbids what God commands, we must obey God rather than the state (Acts 5:29). Our allegiance first is to King Jesus and not to governments, if those governments command us to do what King Jesus forbids. This does not mean that we are to suffer persecution in silence. Jesus called Herod "that fox" (Luke 13:32) and John the Baptist rebuked Herod for his immorality (Mark 6:18). Paul stood his ground against the illegal procedures in his hearing before the Sanhedrin (Acts 23:3). We may criticize the state, but we must do so according to our calling as Christ's disciples. As the church, we call people to repentance and faith, and we call the state to her proper role in God's economy. However, the church must never forget that she is "in" the world but not "of" it (John 17:15-19). The nations of this world-order are reserved for judgment; in light of this, the church is to be the church as nations come and go.

Until Christ returns, Christians must continue to serve in every domain of life, including the state. In democratic governments, where Christians have voices in government, we have a responsibility to participate. In such a situation, the church is to have a prophetic role by perceiving and exposing ethical questions that underlie political issues. The church is not to remain silent on these issues because we are to call all people to know and obey God their Creator and Lord. At the same time, Christians involved in political life must not forget that the church is not the state. Calling the state to righteousness and justice does not mean calling it to promote the gospel with political power. Christians are not free to form an exclusively Christian political party that seeks to exercise power for Christ. Patriotism is misguided that sees any nation as a "Christian nation" and entitled to God's favor and blessing. Ultimately, we must never forget that salvation does not come by the "redemption" of the political order, but by new birth that brings sinners into the church and thus into God's kingdom.

Third, where does Toronto Baptist Seminary fit in this discussion? The role of the seminary is to function as an arm of the church. The calling of a theological seminary is to help the church prepare men and women for gospel ministry, which involves the proclamation and defense of the Christian faith in the world. The seminary has a vital role to help the church by training leaders for the church so that those leaders can serve God's people by seeing them grow in their Christian lives and conformity to Christ. Apart from the faithful work of the seminary, churches will suffer and not be all they can be. But the seminary must remember that she is here to serve the church and by serving the church train a new generation of faithful ministers of the gospel to proclaim Christ, who alone is the hope of the world.

Concluding Reflection

"Desiring a better country." On the occasion of the 150th anniversary of Canada and the 90th anniversary of Toronto Baptist Seminary, we are reminded that as Christians we are to live as citizens of Canada but that our ultimate allegiance is to Christ and his church.

Our responsibility as Canadian Christians is to pray for another 150 years of favor for Canada, if the Lord tarries, but also to never forget that unless the gospel takes hold once again in Canada, our allegiance to Christ will be increasingly tested. Over the last 150 years, we have enjoyed the blessing of living in Canada, but those blessings are only the result of the primary and secondary effects of the gospel. Despite what the future holds, as God's people, we are called to live out what we are in Christ to the glory of our triune God.

On the occasion of these two anniversaries, we must never forget that our greatest need is to know our triune God better in saving relationship with him, and as the church, to really be the church. Nations will come and go. While nations remain, we are called to pray for our leaders and to act as Christian citizens. However, our true hope must never be placed in a nation but in Christ alone and this must be our most fundamental desire: the "better country" of the new creation. It is only in Christ's return that all things will be made right, and it is only in the new creation that the true purpose of our creation will be realized—to dwell forever in the presence of "the LORD God Almighty and the Lamb" (Rev. 21:22). "Amen. Come, Lord Jesus" (Rev. 22:20).

5

DESIRING A BETTER COUNTRY

Glendon G. Thompson

"But now they desire a better, that is, a heavenly country. Therefore God is not ashamed to be called their God, for he has prepared a city for them"
Hebrews 11:16

The statement "They desire a better country" adorning the Canadian coat of arms suggests that Hebrew 11:16 may in some sense apply to this nation. Despite Canada's signal advantages, such as its spectacular beauty, considerable wealth, and enviable security, the "better country" the anonymous pastor refers to in his "word of exhortation" (13:22) transcends this earthly sphere.

The book of Hebrews addresses Christians in the throes of an alarming spiritual crisis. Apparently, some were "slipping into a nominal Christianity"[1] by hankering after the good old days of Judaism. They seemed drawn by the magnetic pull of its temple, the ritual pomp of its priesthood, and the solemn atmosphere of its sacrifices. In order to convince his audience to reverse course, the writer compares all they possessed in Judaism to Christ and concludes that Christ is infinitely superior.

---

[1] I. Howard Marshall, *The Work of Christ* (Carlisle: The Paternoster Press, 1994), 90.

Consequently, he warns against drifting into irretrievable apostasy (6:4-8; 10:26-31)[2] and encourages them to persevere in hardship, just as they did at the onset of their Christian experience when they "endured a great struggle with suffering" (10:32).

The writer does not view perseverance in Christ as automatic. He discloses that believers endure by faith (cf. 10:38). This assertion leads into to an extended discussion on the theme of faith, which occurs eighteen times in chapter 11:1-40. In essence, the chapter covers the distinctive stages in salvation-history, from the earliest heroes of faith (11:3-7) to those who lived from the period of the judges until the advent of the Lord Jesus Christ (11:32-38). This recital of the heroes and heroines of faith underscores a central truth: faith represents the singular means by which all God's people, from the dawn of time, persevere in allegiance to him.

The writer reserves ample space for Abraham and his descendants (11:8-22). In his discourse on Abraham's faith, he

---

[2] *Apostasy* denotes the deliberate and permanent rejection of the faith once formerly professed. Without rehashing earlier reflections on the subject of apostasy (see *The Gospel Witness*, 85, no.12 [May 2007], 7-10) we contend that Hebrews does not support the notion that genuine believers can apostatize from the faith (cf. 2:11; 6:9; 8:10; 9:14; 10:23). However, two additional yet brief observations seem in order. First, the writer discusses apostasy, but not abstractly. He engages real people in a real historical context, at a crossroad in their spiritual journey. Second, the writer describes those in danger of apostasy *phenomenologically* (i.e., from the vantage point of the observer). He warns those who seem to possess the signs of spiritual life, yet were refusing to progress in spiritual maturity. The caution is not against losing salvation, but rather, against turning from Christ, which would prove that their faith is spurious or transitory. See especially, D. A. Carson "Reflections of Assurance" in Thomas Schreiner, Bruce Ware (eds.), *Still Sovereign: Contemporary Perspectives on Election, Foreknowledge, and Grace* (Grand Rapids, MI: Baker Book House Company, 1995), 247-276.

includes the central section (11:13-16) to demonstrate that the patriarchs shared the same forward-looking, eschatological faith as their father, Abraham. He rounds off the pericope with the summary statement: "But now they desire a better, that is, a heavenly country. Therefore God is not ashamed to be called their God, for He has prepared a city for them" (11:16).

Verse 16 depicts the country for which the patriarchs longed intensely as "better," precisely because of its heavenly character. But what is the nature of this better, heavenly country?

The Ultimate Goal of Pilgrimage

First, the better country for which the patriarchs yearned represents the ultimate goal of pilgrimage. Verse 13 contains a telling observation regarding the faith of Abraham, Sarah, Isaac, and Jacob: "These all died in faith, not having received the promises, but having seen them afar off were assured of them, embraced them and confessed that they were strangers and pilgrims on the earth." Bruce elucidates, "Their lives were regulated by the firm conviction that God would fulfill the promise He had given them, and in death, they continued to look forward to the fulfillment of these promises."[3] Although the patriarchs died before they realized the promise of land, innumerable descendants, and blessing to the world, they nevertheless continued to trust in the Lord, beholding from a distance and greeting the promises. At the same time, they were confessing that they were strangers and pilgrims on the earth (11:13).

The concepts "strangers" and "pilgrims" constitute a hendiadys—they form a singular idea. Together, they signify that the patriarchs regarded themselves as temporary residents

---

[3] F. F. Bruce, *Hebrews* (Grand Rapids, MI: W. B. Eerdmans Publishing Co., 1985), 303.

on earth. Although they received the promise of land from God, they consciously determined to live in Canaan as sojourners, without the privileges of citizenship. The fact that they accepted temporary resident status suggests that the patriarchs considered themselves a people in transit to their true home. Verse 14 supports this reading, for it explains that by declaring themselves sojourners in a foreign land, the patriarchs explicitly manifested their determined search for a "homeland."[4] Verse 15 rules out Mesopotamia as the particular homeland that they sought since they had adequate opportunity to return to it if they desired to do so (11:15).

The patriarchs reckoned themselves as resident aliens in Canaan primarily because of the influence of Abraham: "By faith he dwelt in the land of promise as in a foreign country, dwelling in tents with Isaac and Jacob, the heirs with him of the same promise" (11:9). Abraham received the divine call to abandon his most natural attachments, indeed, the pillars of human trust: nation (Ur in Mesopotamia); religious allegiance (moon god); and ethnic roots (Sethite tribe and Terahite clan). When he arrived in Canaan, he refused to put down permanent roots, opting instead for a transient lifestyle in moveable tents. Apart from a burial site, he owned not even a foot of ground in Canaan (Acts 7:5). His alienation from the culture stemmed from the realization that the prosperity God promised him exceeded finite territory on the Mediterranean shore.[5]

---

[4] Lane argues against this view on the ground that the verb epizēteō ("long for") carries no sense of movement towards a place. However, while the term does not literally refer to pilgrimage, it may well do so figuratively. See William L. Lane, *Hebrews 9–13* (Waco, TX: Word Books, 1991), 358.

[5] John Anthony Jelinek, "The Contribution of the City Metaphor: Toward an Understanding of the New Jerusalem" (ThD dissertation, Grace Theological Seminary, 1992), 157.

Lane correctly states that "The yearning of the patriarchs for a country of their own is a witness *to the Christian community* of the reality of a heavenly homeland,"[6] and simultaneously, invites believers to embrace a life of pilgrimage. That Hebrews pictures Christians as a pilgrim people cannot be successfully challenged.[7] The metaphor of movement runs as a scarlet thread throughout the epistle. For example, chapters 3:14-4:11 focuses on the wilderness generation's tragic forfeiture of rest because of their unbelief. The promise of entering into rest remains, but believers must fear, lest they come short of it (4:1). The rest envisioned is none other than the *sabbatismos*, the eschatological rest (4:9). Additionally, the journey vocabulary surfaces in the call for believers to approach: "Let us draw near with a true heart in full assurance of faith, having our hearts sprinkled from an evil conscience and our bodies washed with pure water" (10:22). Moreover, the journey motif appears in the appeals to advance: "Therefore, since we are surrounded by so great a cloud of witnesses, let us lay aside every weight and the sin which so easily ensnares us, and let us run with endurance the race that is set before us" (12:1) and, "Therefore let us go forth to him, outside the camp, bearing his reproach. For here we have no continuing city, but we seek the one to come" (13:13-14).

Paradoxically, the better country for which these patriarchs hungered belongs to the future, but at the same time, it is present. Hebrews thus construes the kingdom of God in terms of "the now and the not yet." Believers have already come to it (12:22). The perfect tense, *proseleuthate*, "have come" indicates present citizenship in the heavenly realm: "The expected latter-

---

[6] Lane, *Hebrews 9-13*, 319. Italics the author's.

[7] See the first major treatment of the pilgrimage motif in Hebrews by Ernest Käsemann, *The Wandering People of God: An Investigation of the Letter to the Hebrews* (Minneapolis: Augsburg, 1984).

day city of God has invaded invisibly into the present age in order that saints may now be able to participate in it."[8] In a real sense, then, the last days have already begun with the coming of Christ, which is the "primary eschatological event...ushered in by the incarnation, death, and ascension of Jesus."[9] However, believers have not yet received all God promised, but anticipate the consummation.

The Essential Quality of Permanence

Second, the better country upon which the patriarchs set their hearts bears the essential quality of permanence. Hebrews betrays a cosmological dualism in which the earthly signifies the inferior and the heavenly the superior.[10] This is especially true in Hebrews 11:13-16. The patriarchs estimated the heavenly country more valuable, and consequently more desirable (11:16) than the land where they had sojourned. But why did they assess it the better country? Briefly stated, for the very reason Abraham did so: "For he waited for the city which has foundations, whose builder and maker *is* God" (11:10). Abraham looked expectantly

---

[8] G. K. Beale, *John's Use of the Old Testament in Revelation* (Sheffield: Sheffield Academic Press, 1998), 141.

[9] C. K. Barrett, "The Eschatology of the Epistle to the Hebrews" in W. D. Davies, D. Daube, and Charles Harold Dodd (eds.), *The Background of the New Testament and its Eschatology* (Cambridge: Cambridge University Press, 1964), 364.

[10] Cf. David A DeSilva, "Entering God's Rest: Eschatology and the Socio-Rhetorical Strategy of Hebrews," *Trinity Journal,* 21 (2000): 28-29. Admittedly, the nature of Hebrews' cosmology is complex; however, Edward Adams' conclusion that the "cosmological ethos" of Hebrews is "decidedly pro-creational," seems overdrawn. "The Cosmology of Hebrews" in Richard Bauckham, Daniel R. Driver, Trevor A. Hart, and Nathan MacDonald (eds.), *The Epistle to the Hebrews and Christian Theology* (Grand Rapids, MI: W. B. Eerdmans Publishing Co., 2009), 139.

for a stable, secure, and permanent city. The nominative "foundations" underscores the inherent reliability of the heavenly city. Abraham and the patriarchs expected the better, immovable city designed and built by God.

Hebrews also emphasizes the stability of the heavenly city by labeling it the unshakable kingdom: "Therefore, since we are receiving a kingdom which cannot be shaken, let us have grace, by which we may serve God acceptably with reverence and godly fear" (12:28). The term "unshakeable" throws into sharp relief the transient material universe described in Hebrews 12:25:

> See that you do not refuse him who speaks. For if they did not escape who refused him who spoke on earth, much more shall we not escape if we turn away from him who speaks from heaven, whose voice then shook the earth; but now he has promised, saying, "Yet once more I shake not only the earth but also heaven."

DeSilva comments illuminatingly:

> Unlike the earthly Jerusalem, prey to all manner of violence, corruption, and profanation throughout history, this heavenly city truly does "have foundations" that will not be shaken. Indeed that city's foundations will enable it alone to stand after the eschatological "shaking" that will destroy every earthly city along with the removal of the visible cosmos itself.[11]

The pastor stresses the fleeting nature of this creation elsewhere. He lays out the case for Jesus' superiority to angels by contrasting the eternality of Christ with the transitory creation:

---

[11] DeSilva, "Entering God's Rest," 35.

> You, Lord, in the beginning laid the foundation of the earth, and the heavens are the work of your hands. They will perish, but you remain; and they will all grow old like a garment; like a cloak you will fold them up, and they will be changed. But you are the same, and your years will not fail (1:10–12; cf. Ps. 102:25–27).

In summary, the patriarchs desired the better country because, unlike this physical creation that the Lord will shake and change, it remains for eternity because of its solid foundations.

The Locus of God's Immediate Presence
More significantly, the better country of the patriarchs serves as the locus of God's immediate presence. Hebrews 11:16b discloses the upshot of the yearning for the better country: "Therefore God is not ashamed to be called their God, for he has prepared a city for them." The Lord who acknowledged that he is their God, designed and constructed a city to display his glory and love, and deliberately suited it to the eternal happiness of his children. This heavenly city, though invisible, exists concretely without any relation to Plato's abstract world of ideas.[12]

DeSilva rightly defines the prepared city as "God's country, the place where God has always been and where God's presence is known in its fullness and not in any dim reflection."[13] Hebrews 12:22–24 conveys the distinct idea that God's glorious presence distinguishes the heavenly city:

> But you have come to Mount Zion and to the city of the living God, the heavenly Jerusalem, to an innumerable company of angels, to the general assembly and church of the firstborn *who are* registered in heaven, to

---

[12] Adams, "The Cosmology of Hebrews," 134.
[13] DeSilva, "Entering God's Rest," 27.

God the Judge of all, to the spirits of just men made perfect, to Jesus the Mediator of the new covenant, and to the blood of sprinkling that speaks better things than *that of* Abel.

These verses reveal the inestimable privilege of New Covenant believers in their unfettered access to the presence of God. They belong to Mount Zion, the heavenly Jerusalem, strikingly portrayed as "the city of the living God," i.e. the polis that belongs to God and the place where he dwells. The additional details of heaven populated by an innumerable company of angels in festal gathering and the Church of the firstborn, flesh out the heavenly scene. However, the entire paragraph revolves around God the judge at the centre of the heavenly community and the Lord Jesus Christ, whose blood speaks better things than the blood of Abel (12:24). His blood accomplishes greater things than the blood of Abel because it cries to God for mercy, not justice, and empowers believers to approach God. The blood of Jesus accomplishes all this by redeeming from sin, cleansing the conscience, and opening "the new and living way" to God. Having offered his superior sacrifice, in "the greater and more perfect tabernacle, not made with hands, that is not of this creation" (9:11), Jesus now resides in the heavenly city, at the right hand of the Majesty on High (1:3), where he performs his Priestly work of representation "in the presence of God for us" (9:24).

Thus, the pastor, like the apostle Paul, conceives of the better country or the heavenly city as pre-eminently the "state of immediate vision of and perfect communion with God and Christ."[14]

---

[14] Geerhaardus Vos, *Redemptive History and Biblical Interpretation: The Shorter Writings of Geerhardus Vos* (Phillipsburg, NJ: Presbyterian and Reformed Publishing Co., 1980), 55.

Conclusion

In conclusion, Hebrews depicts Christians as temporary residents on earth, journeying by faith to the better country. As such, believers should never forget the location of their true country, which is heaven. Vos amplifies this point: "The central abode of the redeemed will be in heaven, although the renewed earth will remain accessible to them and part of the inheritance."[15]

Furthermore, believers are essentially a people on the way; this reality demands, at a minimum, separation from the world and forward movement in faith and godliness. John Bunyan's allegory, *Pilgrim's Progress*, vividly captures the idea that pilgrimage to heaven demands movement.

Since permanence characterizes the better country, believers should invest in the heavenly country and not in material possessions. True security lies in the unshakable realm from where the Lord Jesus will return at the last day, not as an unknown Messiah, but the Jesus who has already lived a human life (9:28).[16] We should do all within our powers to promote the heavenly city because labors for the heavenly abode are not in vain.[17]

The prospect of a better country where God and the Lamb dwell encourages joyful anticipation on the part of Christians. Augustine saw clearly that the heavenly abode consists of God's reward, which is God himself, who is the best and greatest of all possessions.[18] The better country is Yahweh Shammah.

---

[15] Vos, *Redemptive History and Biblical Interpretation*, 55.

[16] Barrett, "The Eschatology of the Epistle to the Hebrews," 363.

[17] Cf. Lane, *Hebrews 9–13*, 359.

[18] Cf. Henry Bettenson, trans., *Saint Augustine, The City of God* (London: Penguin Books Ltd., 2003), 1088.

Contributors

Kevin N. Flatt

Dr. Kevin N. Flatt is Associate Professor of History at Redeemer University College, where he also chairs the Department of History, Politics, and International Studies and serves as the university's Director of Research. He is the author of *After Evangelicalism: The Sixties and the United Church of Canada* (McGill-Queen's University Press, 2013) and several scholarly articles on the history and sociology of Protestantism in Canada. His column appears in each issue of *Faith Today*, Canada's national evangelical magazine. He and his wife Alicia and their two children live in his hometown of Kitchener, Ontario.

Michael A.G. Haykin

Dr. Michael Haykin is Professor of Church History at the Southern Baptist Theological Seminary, Louisville, Kentucky and is the Director of The Andrew Fuller Center for Baptist Studies, which is based in the Southern campus but which also has an office in Ontario. He is the author of a number of books dealing with Patristic and Baptist studies and he is also the general editor of a forthcoming 16-volume edition of the works of Andrew Fuller (Walter de Gruyter). He and his wife Alison have their home in Dundas, Ontario.

Glendon G. Thompson

Dr. Glendon G. Thompson serves as senior pastor of Jarvis Street Baptist Church. He is also the president of and a professor of systematic theology at Toronto Baptist Seminary and Bible College. Dr. Thompson is the editor of The Gospel Witness magazine and is a regular conference speaker and lecturer in Canada, the USA, and the Caribbean.

Kirk Wellum

Kirk Wellum is the Principal of Toronto Baptist Seminary where he also teaches systematic and pastoral theology. Before coming to Toronto Baptist Seminary, he planted a church in Sarnia and served in pastoral ministry in Ontario for 24 years. He regularly speaks in churches and at conferences and has contributed to a number of books, magazines, and journals. He and his wife Debbie have 4 children and 3 grandchildren and have their home in Ancaster, Ontario.

Stephen J. Wellum

Dr. Stephen J. Wellum is Professor of Christian Theology at The Southern Baptist Theological Seminary and editor of *Southern Baptist Journal of Theology*. He received his PhD from Trinity Evangelical Divinity School and he is the author of numerous essays and articles. Dr. Wellum is the co-author with Peter J. Gentry of *Kingdom through Covenant, 2nd edition* (Crossway, 2012, 2018) and *God's Kingdom through God's Covenants: A Concise Biblical Theology* (Crossway, 2015); the author of *God the Son Incarnate: The Doctrine of the Person of Christ* (Crossway, 2016) and *Christ Alone—The Uniqueness of Jesus as Savior* (Zondervan, 2017); and the co-author of *Christ from Beginning to End: How the Full Story of Scripture Reveals the Full Glory of Christ* (Zondervan, 2018). Dr. Wellum was born and raised in Burlington, Ontario. He is married to Karen and together they have five children.

Scripture Index

Genesis
1:26–30 97
1:26–31 94
1:31 96
1–3 95
2 94
3 96
3:15 .... 71, 95, 97, 101
6:8 97
6:18 97
6–9 97
8:1 108
8:21 98
8:22 97
9:1–7 97
9:6 98
9:9–17 97
10 98
11 98
12:1–3 103
12:1–3 .... 99, 101
15 100
15:4–5 99
17:1–8 99
18:18–19 99
22:16–18 99

Exodus
2:24–25 101
3:40 102
3:6 101
4:22–23 .... 102, 104

19:6 103
19:4 101
19:5–6 101
25:9 102

Numbers
11:27–29 107
16 73
22:23 74
22–25:3 73
24:15–19 79
31 74
31:8 73

Deuteronomy
4:36–38 101
7:7 101
7:8 101
10:16 107
30:6 107

1 Samuel
1:19 108

2 Samuel
7:12–16 104
7:14 104
7:19b 104
7:22–24 104

1 Kings
16 77
21 77

2 Kings
9 77
13:22–23 101

1 Chronicles
16:15-19 101
19. Psalms
2 .... 76, 78, 104, 105
8 .... 94, 105
16:11 22
45 105
47:9 106
67:2-3 106
72 105
72:8 .... 91, 92
87:3-6 106
89:26-27 104
102:25-27 126
110 108
117:1 106
Isaiah
7:14 105
9:6-7 105
9:6-7, 11, 53 105
11:1 79
11:1-10 105
11:1-3 107
14:1-2 106
19:23-25 106
22:2—22 81
42:1-9 105
42:6, 20 106
49:1-2 107
49:1-7 105
49:6 106
52:13-53:12 105

55:3 105
55:3-5 106
56:4-8 106
61:1 107
61:1-3 106
65:17 106
66:18-24 106
66:22 106
Jeremiah
4:4 107
9:25 107
16:19 106
23:5-6 106
31:29-34 106
31:31-34 107
31:31-40 106
31:33-34 .... 107, 108
31:34 106
32:39 110
33:6-16 106
33:9 106
33:14-26 106
Ezekiel
11:19 110
11:19-20 107
34:23-24 106
36:24-38 106
36:25-27 107
36:36 106
37:11-28 106
37:24-28 106
37:28 106

Daniel
3 76
Hosea
11:1 104
Joel
2:28–32 .... 106, 107
Amos
9:11–12 106
Zechariah
4:6 83
Matthew
2:15 71
11:29 23
16:13–20 .... 83, 111
16:18 114
16:19 110
18:15–20 111
28:18–20 111
Mark
6:18 116
12:13–17 115
Luke
3:38 102
13:32 116
John
1:29 23
8:39–44 71
17:15–19 116
Acts
2 107
5:29 116
7:5 122

19 66
20:28–30 67
23:3 116
Romans
2:28–29 71
2:29 107
3:23 95
5:12–21 96
9:6 108
9:6–24 71
13:1–2 115
13:1–7 .... 93, 98
Galatians
3:16 100
4:21–31 71
6:16 71
Ephesians
2:11–22 114
3:7–13 114
Philippians
2 24
2:6–11 71
2:7–8 23
2:15–16 69
3:20 110
Colossians
1:13 110
1:15–20 71
1:17 .... 23, 24
1 Timothy
1:15 67
4:1–8 67

6:2–3 68	12:25 125

2 Timothy
- 3:1–9 68
- 3:10–4:5...................... 68

Titus
- 3:1 115

Hebrews
- 1:3 23
- 2:5–18......................... 108
- 5:1 102
- 7:11 102
- 8–9 102
- 10:4 108
- 10:17 108
- 11:6 91
- 11:10 124
- 11:10, 16.................... 110
- 11:13–16.................... 124
- 11:16 ....1, 24, 92, 96, 119
- 11:16b....................... 126
- 12:18–29.................... 109
- 12:22 123
- 12:22–24.................... 126
- 12:25 125
- 12:28 ....110, 125
- 13:14 ....109, 110

2 Peter
- 3:13 96

Revelation
- 1:9–20......................... 65
- 1:13–15....................... 76
- 2:1–7 68
- 2–3 ....63, 76
- 3:7 110
- 5:6 23
- 5:8 22
- 5:14 22
- 7:11 22
- 13:11–17...................... 77
- 13–14......................... 116
- 17:14 22
- 19:16 22
- 21:22 118
- 21:23 23
- 22:16 79
- 22:20 118

Date Completed	Name

H&E *Publishing*

www.HesedAndEmet.com

www.ingramcontent.com/pod-product-compliance
Lightning Source LLC
Chambersburg PA
CBHW030910080526
44589CB00010B/234